Prevention of Sports Injuries
A Biomechanical Approach

Carole Zebas, P.E.D.
Department of Health, Physical
Education and Recreation
University of Kansas

Michael Chapman, P.T., M.S.
Department of Physical Therapy
Co-Director of Sports Clinic Medicine
University of Kansas

D1716759

eb
eddie bowers publishing, inc.
2600 Jackson Street
Dubuque, Iowa 52001

Acknowledgments

Several people have contributed to the completion of this project. We would like to acknowledge Liz and Dave (the "Wordoctors"); Bruce and Johncy (photography); and Russ (graphics).

Those who provided both constructive criticism and moral support were: Vickie, Nancy, Mardi, Jackie, and Yvonne for Carole, and Karen and Sandy for Michael.

Finally, there are those family members who inspired us to continue, and understood when the project took away time we usually have for them; Nick and Joanne for Carole, and Dan for Michael.

Thank you all.

Book Design and Production
David Corona Design

eddie bowers publishing company
2600 Jackson Street
Dubuque, Iowa 52001

ISBN 0–945483–01–5

Copyright © 1990 by eddie bowers publishing company

All rights reserved. No part of this publication may be reproduced, stored in a retrieval system, or transmitted, in any form or by any means, electronic, mechanical, photocopy, recording or otherwise, without the prior written permission of eddie bowers publishing company.

Printed in the United States of America

9 8 7 6 5 4 3 2 1

Contents

114149

Chapter 7 . . . . page 130

Specific Injury Prevention Methods

Chapter 8 . . . . . . page 152

The Rehabilitation Process

Chapter 9 . . . . . . page 158

Drugs and Environmental Conditions

Relating to Sports Injury

List of Figures

List of Tables

Prevention of Sports Injuries

A Biomechanical Approach

Introduction and Terminology

Philosophy of Sport Injury Prevention

The emphasis on prevention of injury in sport and exercise has been increasing in recent years. A review of resources indicates that prevention efforts are occurring for a wide variety of exercise activities and sports. This new level of interest in prevention crosses not only different sports, but different age groups and competition levels. A physician and author who has written on sports injuries for many years writes, "Actually, there have been many developments in medicine and in health care of the athlete, with a change in emphasis, particularly among the public and school personnel who have been much more conscious of prevention than ever before." (O'Donaghue, 1984)

The fitness boom which started in the seventies (and seems to be continuing) is complemented by the wellness boom of the eighties. Therefore, the numbers of people involved in exercise and sport continue to increase. People of all ages are becoming involved, from the very young preschoolers in soccer programs to the senior age nursing home residents in exercise programs.

Along with this increase in interest in fitness and activity, there is a greater potential for injury. Concurrently there is a new impatience with limiting activity during recovery from an injury. This change in attitude significantly complicates the prevention of activity related injuries. Just a few years ago people would more readily take their doctor's suggestion to rest and/or permanently change their participation level or activity. People are now seeking advice which is tailored to reduce their recovery time and get them "back in the game" as soon as possible. Although this philosophy is certainly not new for competitive athletes, it is new for the cross section of humanity that expects this approach to their injuries today.

As part of a new prevention of injury effort, there are excellent examples of changes in rules, such as the blocking rules of football, as well as changes in philosophy of training. "No pain-no gain" has been replaced by "Train, but don't strain" for many sports, particularly for general fitness programs of unsupervised individuals. A greater understanding of the anatomy and physiology of the human body has done away with many poor and even dangerous practices. The bounce stretch, complete immobilization of joints post surgically, and water deprivation during team sport workouts, are a few classic examples of practices that are now changed. Remember that as late as the 1960's these practices were almost universally accepted as good injury prevention, training or rehabilitation techniques. One has to wonder what we are now doing that will be changed to benefit our athletes and fitness programs in the future.

Through a better understanding of the human body, improvements in equipment, training, and changes in rules of competition, we are getting better at reducing the number and severity of initial injuries. Certainly this is progress, and the most desired type of prevention. However, there are two other kinds of prevention that are also important to consider. One of these is the prevention of extending a preexisting injury, or allowing it to get worse through poor management or rehabilitation efforts. The other kind of prevention is to reduce the detraining effect that occurs with injury, thus preventing needless delay in return to activity.

If one is to make progress in all areas of prevention, then it becomes imperative to know more about how specific tissues react to the variety of stresses that activity provides, as well as how body parts interact to accomplish functional motion. An understanding of sports injuries from this approach requires an understanding of biomechanics. "Biomechanics" is defined in several ways, but the definition that will be used in this text is "... biomechanics is the study of forces, and effects of those forces on the human body." (LeVeau, 1977).

Basic Biomechanical Terminology and Concepts

To facilitate the understanding of biomechanics as it relates to sport and exercise injury, a list of terms and concepts is provided. Definitions for terms are given and explanations of concepts are described. Where appropriate, examples are used to clarify. More detailed explanations will be given in ensuing chapters. This section is divided into categories of mechanics, kinematics, linear kinetics, angular kinetics, Newton's Laws of Motion, muscle mechanics, and non- contractile tissue mechanics.

Mechanics

Mechanics, broadly defined, is the branch of physics which deals with motion and how internal and external forces on a body influence that motion. Biomechanics implies the body is a living one.

Biomechanics can be divided into statics and dynamics. Statics is the study of nonmoving bodies, while dynamics is the study of moving bodies. The study of dynamics is divided further into kinematics and kinetics. Kinematics describes a body in terms of velocities and accelerations (how fast a body moves), distances and displacements (how far a body moves), and time (how long it takes a body to move). Kinetics describes the forces which act on a body (what causes motion to occur).

Kinematics

The following definitions or concepts are those most associated with a sport/exercise injury. This is by no means a complete list of kinematic terms.

Velocity. Velocity is the rate at which a body moves from one point to another. If the body is moving in a straight line, the velocity is linear. When the body rotates about an axis, the velocity is angular/rotary. Speed sometimes is used as a synonym for velocity. However, there is a distinct difference between velocity and speed. Velocity is a vector which means it is expressed in magnitude and direction. Speed is a scalar which means it has magnitude only.

$$\text{velocity} = \frac{\text{change in displacement}}{\text{change in time}}$$

$$\text{angular velocity} = \frac{\text{change in angle}}{\text{change in time}}$$

Velocity is usually expressed in such units as ft/s, m/s, mph, etc. Angular velocity can be expressed as deg/s, rev/s, rad/s.

EXAMPLE: The velocity/speed of a body, body segment, object has a direct relationship upon its impact with another body or object.

Acceleration. Acceleration is the rate of change of velocity with respect to time. Because it is a vector it can be expressed in positive, negative, or zero values. Acceleration may be linear or angular.

$$\text{acceleration} = \frac{\text{change in velocity}}{\text{change in time}}$$

$$\text{angular acceleration} = \frac{\text{change in angular velocity}}{\text{change in time}}$$

Acceleration is usually expressed as ft/s/s, or m/s/s; whereas, angular acceleration is expressed as deg/s/s, or rad/s/s.

EXAMPLE: A pitcher must accelerate his arm to produce speed on the ball, and then he must decelerate or "slow down" his arm at the follow through of the pitch. Otherwise, the tremendous forces on the elbow and shoulder may cause an injury to occur.

Acceleration of objects toward the earth due to gravitational forces is 32 ft/s/s or 9.8 m/s/s. Technically, these values will change slightly depending on the location of the body in space.

Kinetics

Kinetics describes the causes of motion, namely forces. This is a key concept in the discussion of injury evaluation, treatment, and prevention.

Mass and Weight. Mass is described as a quantity of matter. It can be determined by dividing the weight of a body by the acceleration of a body due to gravitational force. It is considered to be a constant rather than a variable because it does not change when location in space is altered. Weight sometimes is substituted for mass; however, the two terms are different. Weight is the gravitational force acting on a body drawing it toward the center of the earth. It is a variable quantity because it changes its value when location in space is changed.

$$mass = \frac{weight}{gravity} \qquad weight = mass \times gravity$$

Inertia. Inertia can be described best as a reluctance to change the current state of being. A body that is moving has a resistance or a reluctance to change position. Likewise, a body that is not moving resists a change to a moving condition. A measure of inertia is the mass of the body.

Force. A force is a push or pull that changes the current state of being. If a body is at rest, an applied force will cause the body to move. If the body is moving, a force may cause it to change directions, slow down, speed up, or stop moving. Forces also can cause objects to deform. Muscles are considered to be internal body forces. Gravity, friction, air, and water are examples of external forces acting upon the body.

A force is a vector in that it has magnitude and direction. In order to fully understand how forces affect a body, it is necessary to know: (a) the magnitude of the force; (b) the line and direction; and (c) the point of application. (See Figure 1.1)

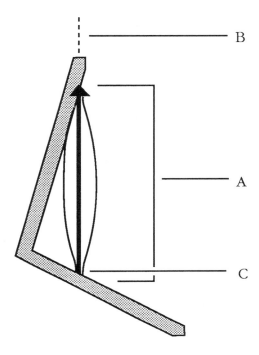

Figure 1.1.
Force vector: (A) magnitude of force; (B) line and direction of force;
(C) point of application.

      Friction. Friction is a force which modifies motion, and works parallel
(tangential) to the surfaces of the two objects involved. Friction may be dry or
wet, sliding or rolling. The amount of dry, sliding friction developed depends upon
the normal reaction force (forces holding the two surfaces together),and the nature
of surfaces that are interfacing with each other (a constant). This is known as
the Law of Friction. Limiting friction is that instant just before movement begins.

$$\text{limiting friction} = \frac{\text{constant}}{\text{normal reaction}}$$

Wet and rolling limiting friction are less than dry, sliding friction.

      The coefficient of friction is an indicator of the amount of friction between
the surfaces. It has a range of 0 to 1. If the coefficient is 0, a frictionless state
exists. Some common coefficients of friction are (Williams and Lissner, 1977;
White and Panjabi, 1978):

rubber on dry concrete	0.60–0.70
dry metal on dry metal	0.15–0.20
cartilage on cartilage in an animal ankle joint	0.005

Pressure. Pressure describes how forces are distributed over an area. If the force is applied over a small area, the pressure is great. If the force is distributed over a greater area, the pressure will be reduced.

$$\text{pressure} = \frac{\text{force}}{\text{area}}$$

Pressure is expressed as pounds per square inch (psi), or Newtons per square centimeter (N/cm/cm).

EXAMPLE: If you were to attempt a rescue of a person who had fallen through ice, you certainly would find it a bit more risky to walk out onto the ice in the direction of the victim. Crawling out on the ice on your stomach would distribute your body weight (force) over the area of your entire body.

Work. Work is the result of applying a force over some distance. Technically, the distance the body moves must be in the direction in which the force acts. This definition should be further qualified by calling the work done "mechanical work". Physiological work has another meaning.

$$\text{work} = \text{force x distance}$$

The units of mechanical work are expressed in ft-lbs or joules.

EXAMPLE: Energy is the capacity to do work. Therefore, work and energy have a direct relationship to each other. (See definitions for energy below.) If the distance through which work can be done is reduced, the energy also is reduced. Landing properly from a height takes this relationship into consideration. If the forces can be dissipated over some distance such as in bending the knee, then the impact is less severe in nature.

Power. Power is the rate of doing work. More power is generated if the work can be done in a short amount of time.

$$\text{power} = \frac{\text{work}}{\text{time}}$$

The units of power are ft-lbs/s, horsepower, or watts.

Energy.   Energy is the capacity to do work. In biomechanics, there are three types of energy: kinetic, potential, and strain.

Kinetic Energy .   Kinetic energy is the energy a body possesses because of its motion. It is dependent upon the mass and the velocity of the object.

$$\text{kinetic energy} = 1/2 \text{ mass x velocity}$$

Potential Energy . Potential energy is the energy a body possesses by virtue of its position. In a sense, it is the storage of energy with the capability of being used at some future time. Potential energy is dependent upon the weight of the body and its height above the earth's surface.

$$\text{potential energy} = \text{weight x height}$$

Strain energy.   Strain energy is the work capacity that a body has as a result of being deformed. This term sometimes is used synonymously with potential energy. All units of energy are expressed in ft-lbs or joules.

EXAMPLE: A ligament strain serves as an example for understanding the energy concept. Imagine that the ligament is a rubber band which is being stretched. As the rubber band is stretched it is deformed (strain energy). When the rubber band is stretched as far as it will go, it has the potential to return to its original shape (potential energy). When the stretched rubber band is no longer under tension, it returns to its original shape (kinetic energy).

Angular Kinetics

Angular kinetics describes the causes of motion around an axis. For example, the bones of our body rotate about axes called joints. Much of the forthcoming discussion on angular kinetics will refer to the skeletal system.

Lever. A lever is a simple machine. It is based on the principle that a resistance is moved through a distance by means of a force to produce work. The levers of the human body are the bones of the skeleton.

There are three classes of levers, named for the way in which the parts are arranged. (See Figure 1.2.)

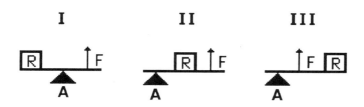

Figure 1.2.
Classes of levers.

Each class of lever has a special function. The Class I lever is designed for balance, force production, or speed/range of motion. The Class II lever favors force while the Class III lever favors speed and/or range of motion. Most of the levers of the human body are Class III levers which allows them to move through large ranges of motion with speed. They are not very effective in moving large loads with a minimum of effort.

Lever arm. The lever arm is the perpendicular distance from the line of force to the axis of rotation. (See Figure 1.3)

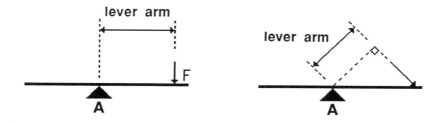

Figure 1.3.
Lever arms.

It also is called a torque arm or a moment arm.

Force Couple. When two forces are equal in magnitude, opposite in direction, and parallel to each other, they form what is known as a force couple. (See Figure 1.4).

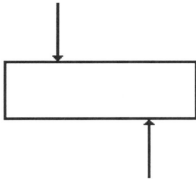

Figure 1.4.
Force couple.

Torque. Torque is the product of the force causing the lever to turn and the torque (lever) arm distance. It describes the "turning effect" of the lever. If the force causing the lever to turn is greater than the force of resistance, the lever will move in the direction of the force. If the resistance force is greater, the lever will move in the direction of the resistance force.

$$torque = force \ x \ torque \ arm \ distance$$

The magnitude of the torque may be changed in one of two ways. First, the magnitude of the force can be changed. Second, the lever arm length can be changed by changing its point of application or changing the force direction. (See Figure 1.5).

$$F \ x \ d_{\perp} \quad or \quad F \ x \ \mathbf{d}_{\perp}$$

Figure 1.5.
Changing torques.

EXAMPLE: In lifting heavy objects from the floor, it is desirable to hold the object close to the body to reduce the torque. Holding the object away from the body causes stress to the vertebrae and soft tissue in the lower back.

Equilibrium.   There may be several torques acting upon one body, i.e., the human body. Some may be moving in a clockwise direction while others are moving in a counterclockwise direction. If the sum of the torques acting on the body is equal to zero, the body is said to be in equilibrium.

Center of Gravity.   The center of gravity of a body has several definitions. It may be considered to be the point at which the body is balanced. It also is considered to be the point where the mass of the body is said to be concentrated. In the anatomical standing position of a human, the center of gravity is located at the junction of the three cardinal planes of the body. In the standing position, this approximately is located just below the navel.

Newton's Laws of Motion

Sir Isaac Newton (1642-1727) was responsible for formulating the laws which govern motion. He summarized these in three sentences.

Newton I.   This law tells us what happens to a body which has not changed its present status. It is stated as:

Every body at rest, or moving with constant velocity in a straight line, will continue in that state unless compelled to change by an external force exerted upon it.

This law also is known as the Law of Inertia.

Newton II.   Newton's second law tells us what happens to a body once a force has been applied to it. It says:

The acceleration of a body is proportional to the force causing it and takes place in the direction in which the force acts.

This law also is known as the Law of Acceleration and is sometimes written as

$$Force = mass \times acceleration$$

Newton III. The third law explains the reaction of a body to force which has been applied to it. It states:

For every force that is exerted by one body on another, there is an equal and opposite force exerted by the second body on the first.

This law also is known as the Law of Reaction.

Momentum. Momentum quantifies motion for us. It is the product of the mass of a body and the velocity with which it is moving.

$$momentum = mass \times velocity$$

Impulse. Impulse is the product of force and time. If we know the impulse, we can quantify the effect of the force on the velocity of a body. This can further be described as a change in momentum and is called the impulse-momentum relationship. This relationship is related to Newton II.

Law of Conservation of Momentum. This Law tells us that total momentum of a system is unaltered no matter what the condition. If for example, two objects collided, the total momentum for the system would be the sum of each of the bodies in the collision. This also is referred to as Newton's First Law of Motion.

Muscle Mechanics

Muscle Action

Muscles act in different ways according to the resistance set against the muscle contraction.

Concentric muscle action. Concentric muscle action involves the shortening of the muscle under tension. This occurs when the external torques acting on the body segment are less than the torque caused by the muscle.

EXAMPLE: The biceps brachii muscle is active in elbow flexion. If the lower arm is flexed toward the shoulder, the muscle action is termed concentric.

Eccentric muscle action. Eccentric muscle action involves the lengthening of the muscle under tension. This occurs when the external torques acting on the body segment are greater than the torque caused by the muscle.

EXAMPLE: If a heavy weight was held in the hand when the elbow was being flexed, and it was causing the elbow to extend instead of flex, the muscle action would be termed eccentric.

Isometric muscle action. This situation exists when no movement occurs because the external resistance to movement is equal to the internal force being produced.

EXAMPLE: A heavy weight that cannot be lifted off the floor.

Length-tension Relationship

Muscles exert the greatest tension when they are at their greatest length. Generally, the length at which this occurs is slightly greater than the resting length of the muscle. As the length is reduced, less tension is developed.

Angle of Pull

One side of the angle is determined by the line of pull of a muscle. The other side of the angle is determined by a line drawn through the joint and segment through which the muscle is inserted. (See Figure 1.6)

Force-velocity Relationship

As the speed of a muscular contraction increases, the force it is able to exert decreases. Maximal force can be exerted when the speed of muscle contraction is zero or isometric. (See Figure 1.7).

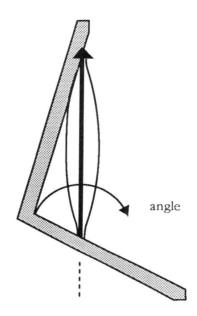

angle

Figure 1.6.
Angle of pull.

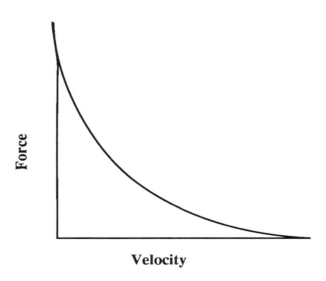

Figure 1.7.
Force-velocity curve.

Stored Elastic Energy

When a muscle is contracted concentrically after having been put on stretch eccentrically, stored elastic energy is released. This provides an additional force to the one provided by the contractile elements of the muscle.

EXAMPLE: If one were to jump from a box to a flexed knee position before jumping straight into the air, the result would be greater than simply jumping straight into the air.

Tissue Mechanics

Elastic-plastic

Elastic action refers to the ability of an object to return to its original shape once it has been deformed. Plastic action refers to the inability of an object to return to its original shape after being deformed.

EXAMPLE: If one performs a static stretching exercise, the ligaments tend to return to their original state after the stretch. If the stretch has been excessive, the ligaments may not be completely restored to their original shape.

Load Application

Three terms are used to explain what happens when a load is placed on an object.

Load. A load is any external force placed upon an object.

Stress. Stress is the internal resistance to the load placed upon an object.

Strain. Strain is the deformation which occurs to an object because of the load placed upon it.

EXAMPLE: If a person was hit on the lateral side of the knee, a load would be applied to the medial collateral ligament. The ligament would resist the the load, but some deformation would occur. If the load was great enough, the ligament would be torn.

Tissue Behavior Under Loading

Bone, tendon, ligament, or cartilage behaves differently depending on the load which has been placed upon it.

Tension or tensile forces. Tension or tensile forces occur when equal and opposite loads are applied outward from the object. (See Figure 1.8)

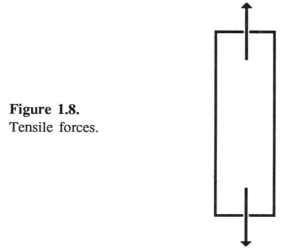

Figure 1.8.
Tensile forces.

EXAMPLE: Tension is placed on the tibial tubercle when the quadriceps are contracted.

Compression forces. Compression forces occur when equal and and opposite loads are applied inward from the object. (See Figure 1.9)

Figure 1.9.
Compression forces.

EXAMPLE: When jumping from a height, the vertebrae in the lower spine are compressed to absorb the shock.

Shear forces. Shear forces occur when parallel loads are applied to the object. (See Figure 1.10)

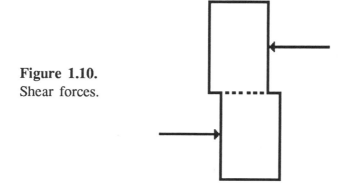

Figure 1.10.
Shear forces.

EXAMPLE: An injury to a young child whose bones have not fully developed may result in the separation of the bone from the epiphyseal plate.

Torsional forces. Torsional forces occur when the object is twisted about its own axis. (See Figure 1.11)

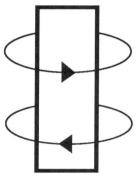

Figure 1.11.
Torsional forces.

EXAMPLE: The medial rotation of the upper arm in arm wrestling may cause a spiral fracture to occur.

Summary

In an effort to prevent injuries there are two basic facts that require understanding. First, there are societal trends toward more activity for all people. This places a great variety and number of participants "in the arena" for the possibility of an injury. Second, there is a vast (and growing) amount of scientific information about the human body that can be used to reduce the risk of injury. It is the task of this book to provide useful, biomechanical information to help educators, coaches, and sports medicine personnel, in the prevention of injuries. This would allow even more people to participate in safe, beneficial, and enjoyable sports and activities.

References

Ellison, A. E. et.al. (Eds.). (1984). Athletic Training and Sports Medicine. Chicago, IL: American Academy of Orthopaedic Surgeons.

Gould, J. A. and G. J. Davies (Eds.). (1985). Orthopaedic and Sports Physical Therapy, Vol. 2. . St. Louis: The C. V. Mosby Company.

LeVeau, B. (1977). Williams and Lissner: Biomechanics of Human Motion. Philadelphia: W. B. Saunders Company.

Nordin, M. and V. H. Frankel. (1989). Basic Biomechanics of the Musculoskeletal System. Philadelphia: Lea & Febiger Publishers.

O'Donohue, D. H. (1984). Treatment of Injuries to Athletes, Fourth Edition. Philadelphia: W. B. Saunders Company.

Rodgers, M. M. and Cavanagh, P. R. (1984, December). "Glossary of Biomechanical Terms, Concepts, and Units". Physical Therapy. 64(12):1886-1902.

White, A. A. and M. M. Panjobi. (1978). Clinical Biomechanics of the Spine. Philadelphia: J.B. Lippincott.

Chapter **2**

A Physician's Concept of Sport and Exercise Participation

Lawrence Magee, M.D., FAAFP, FACSM

Exercise Prescription and Prevention of Injuries
Obesity
Musculoskeletal Abnormalities
Flexibility
Equipment and Surfaces
Medical Illnesses
Environment

Diagnosis of Injuries
Acute
Overuse

Treatment and Rehabilitation of Injuries

Physicians see a large number of sports- or activity-related injuries and problems. In the process of orchestrating the diagnosis, treatment, and prevention of injuries, the use of a biomechanical approach helps to improve the quality of care. This can be seen by evaluating the physician's role in the following areas: 1) exercise prescription and prevention of injuries; 2) diagnosis of injuries, and 3) treatment and rehabilitation of injuries.

Exercise Prescription and Prevention of Injuries

Individuals often seek advice from physicians concerning exercise as it relates to physical conditioning, training for a specific athletic event, rehabilitation from an illness or injury, and weight loss. Since it is much better to prevent injuries when possible rather than to treat them later, this is an opportunity for exercising individuals to benefit from an evaluation of their individual structural characteristics that influence the biomechanical forces involved in exercise. Some of the more common potential problems follow.

Obesity

Overweight individuals place increased deceleration forces on their feet, ankles, knees, and hips because of the increased shock absorption required with repetitive activities. This can lead to injuries of the feet, lower legs, knees, and hips. In addition to counseling on weight loss, these individuals should be advised to use footwear with good shock absorbing characteristics, and exercise on surfaces that have more "give" to them, such as grass vs. concrete. These individuals will also benefit from restricting activities, at least initially, to those activities that produce less severe deceleration forces, such as swimming, bicycling, or walking as opposed to jogging or aerobic dancing.

Musculoskeletal Abnormalities

Foot structure abnormalities, such as excessive pronation or supination, predispose the athlete to certain injuries because of inadequate or abnormal dispersion of the forces encountered by the foot as it makes contact with the exercise surface. Individuals with excessive pronation, because of a relatively flat and overly compliant foot, transmit abnormal rotational forces, up into the lower leg and knee. This may result in injuries to these areas, such as "shin splints" or anterior compartment knee pain. People with excessive supination have a relatively stiff or arched foot, which tends not to absorb the shock of exercise (as well as the excessive pronator), resulting in injuries to the feet, such as stress fractures or plantar fasciitis. This abnormal structure can also influence injuries further up the lower extremities, such as iliotibial band, "shin splints," or stress fractures. (See Chapter 6 for further discussion.)

Leg length discrepancy also can cause altered distribution of the forces of exercise, resulting in knee, hip, and back injuries. Valgus (knock-kneed) or varus (bow-legged) structures of the knee influence the way forces are transmitted or absorbed.

Flexibility

Flexibility plays an important role in injury cause and prevention. A tight muscle group restricts normal range of motion of a joint and alters the forces absorbed or generated through that joint. For example, an inflexible hamstring muscle results in increased compression forces of the patella as it slides across the anterior knee joint, causing increased subpatellar irritation. Inflexibility of the muscles of the lower leg predispose to Achilles tendonitis or anterior leg problems because of altered absorption and transmission of forces. (See Chapter 7 for further discussion.)

An understanding of how these structures and conditions alter the effect of forces involved in exercise allows the physician to better prevent injuries by appropriate intervention. A progressive training program or exercise schedule allows the exercise participant's body to adjust to the increasing forces of exercise. Stretching and strengthening of the appropriate muscle groups decreases the risk of acute injuries and also of overuse injuries. Orthotics may be needed in individuals with structural abnormalities to help correct the altered forces generated by the structures.

Equipment and Surfaces

Equipment used during exercise also may influence development and dispersion of forces. Footwear should provide adequate shock absorption support while not compounding existing structural problems. For example, pronators should wear shoes with good shock absorption and heel support while avoiding shoes with excessive curvature of the last (sole) which should accentuate the pronation. Supinators, on the other hand, may benefit from curved lasts, but still need good shock absorption. Bicycles should be adjusted to decrease forces across the knees (seat height) and the back (handlebar height).

Surfaces or conditions can affect the forces of exercise. Concrete absorbs much less force than surfaces such as grass or suspended floors, therefore resulting in increased force transmission through the lower extremities. Running uphill requires the calf muscle to handle forces at a more elongated length than usual, while running downhill requires more shock absorption to the anterior lower leg and knee.

Medical Illnesses

Medical illnesses or conditions may directly affect the biomechanics of exercise, or indirectly affect the biomechanics of exercise by means of decreased cardio-vascular or pulmonary performance, leading to easier fatigability and decreased performance of the musculoskeletal components that are involved with exercise. Of special concern, because of the increased demands of exercise on the circulatory system and because of the sudden impact with which heart disease can present, is anyone suspected of being at risk for cardiovascular disease. These people should be medically evaluated prior to starting an exercise program. However, medical conditions should not necessarily be considered a contraindication to exercise. Longstanding joint problems (e.g., arthritis) may require less shock-producing activities for exercise such as swimming or bicycling. Exercise may be of benefit in many of these conditions, for example, cardiovascular disease or diabetes, when done with the evaluation and supervision of a physician.

Environment

Environment in terms of heat and/or humidity and cold also influences the body's ability to cope with the forces of exercise, and the athlete will benefit from education in this area. (See Chapter 9 for further discussion.)

Diagnosis of Injuries

When an athlete or exerciser presents with an injury, examination of the injured area with an understanding of the biomechanical forces involved in the injury will aid in the diagnosis. A history of previous injuries of the same type or location may point to a biomechanical predisposition to injury (i.e., laxity of ligaments in the ankle secondary to previous sprains) or an inadequate rehabilitation from a previous injury (i.e., recurrent hamstring strain due to inadequate strengthening and flexibility of the hamstring muscle).

Acute

In an acute (or deceleration) injury, the history of the forces involved during the injury gives valuable information concerning the affected structures. The activity and stance of the athlete (knees bent, falling, sprinting, stopping, changing directions, etc.), conditions of the playing surface (mud, artificial turf, etc.), directions of joint deformity (inversion or eversion of the ankle, varus or valgus motion of the knee, etc.), and external forces applied to the athlete (i.e., contact from another player) are all producers of biomechanical forces affecting the injury. The onset of "popping" or "snapping," pain, swelling or deformity, and their chronological relationship to the injury help to estimate the magnitude of the forces applied and predict the extent of the injury.

The knowledge of the activity required with each exercise or how each sport is played will allow a better understanding of what type of forces athletes are subjected to while participating in that sport. A basketball player undergoes different biomechanical stresses in going up for or coming down from a rebound than a cross-country runner does during a workout. A defensive back tackling a ball carrier is at risk for different injuries to the shoulder than a quarterback passing the football or a tennis player serving. An understanding of the sport involved also allows for better communication with the athlete when discussing the injury, and therefore a better history of the forces involved in the injury.

Overuse

Overuse injuries, or those brought on by repetitive stresses, require investigation of training schedules or exercise habits in terms of amount, frequency, intensity, type of exercise, and any changes in these. Body structure, shoes, surfaces, and coexisting injuries also are important factors as discussed previously. These all affect the repetitive forces that produce overuse injuries, and small changes in a repetitive activity can produce enough cumulative forces to result in injury. Biomechanical abnormalities in terms of structure or secondary to previous or coexisting injury may produce abnormal forces of small enough magnitude to not cause problems with limited exercise but, when repeated numerous times (as in long-distance running), may accumulate to cause clinical injury.

Treatment and Rehabilitation of Injuries

Treatment and rehabilitation of injuries should be thought of together because inadequate rehabilitation is inadequate treatment. In the acute treatment of injuries, any alteration of the biomechanical forces that would result in reduced stress to the injured structure, reduced pain, or reduced swelling should be used. For example, an injured ligament in an ankle sprain should be protected from the forces that have damaged the ligament, or that would reinjure it, by appropriate protection or bracing. Any biomechanical forces that place increased stress on the injured structure should be reduced. An example would be protection of an injured anterior talofibular ligament of the ankle from excessive supination and plantar flexion or protecting a sprain of the medial collateral ligament of the knee from valgus deformity or extreme flexion or extension forces. Overuse injury, such as Achilles tendonitis, responds to a heel lift which decreases the forces (stretching of the tendon) that aggravate it. Injuries caused by excessive pronation of the feet in runners can be treated with the help of footwear and orthotics which redistribute the forces working on the foot, lower leg, and knee. Compressive forces, such as an elastic wrap or elevation of the injured part, help counteract the forces of gravity, therefore reducing swelling, edema and pain, especially when combined with cold therapy.

Early return to protective function when appropriate has been an important advance in the treatment of activity-related injuries. The challenge is to control and orchestrate the forces that, on one hand, would increase the damage or inhibit healing and, on the other hand, maintain strength, flexibility, and function of the injured part. This encourages and allows appropriate complete rehabilitation and return to activity. The rehabilitation includes strengthening to overcome any abnormality in function, either secondary to the injury or preexisting, that contributed to the injury or may cause future problems. For example, in the treatment of a lateral ankle sprain, strengthening of the peroneal muscle and tendon system would guard against further episodes of excessive inversion and supination. Another example would be in the treatment of the anterior compartment syndrome of the knee, or patellar-femoral pain. By increasing the strength of the distal quadriceps muscle (in conjunction with increasing the flexibility of the hamstring muscles), the forces causing stress on the patello-femoral joint are reduced.

The strengthening process also should be used for regaining strength lost because of immobilization or disuse. After casting of an ankle fracture or after knee surgery, there is muscle that has atrophied which requires reeducation and restrengthening to return to complete function.

Lack of flexibility, either existing prior to the injury and therefore a cause of the injury (i.e., hamstring tightness with anterior compartment syndrome of the knee or gastrocnemius tightness with Achilles tendonitis), or as a result of the injury (i.e., quadriceps tightness status post contusion of the quadriceps), is important to correct. A tight, inflexible muscle places abnormal forces on other muscles, tendons and ligaments, predisposing to further injuries.

Appropriate proprioception, or the ability to tell what a part of your body is doing without looking at it, requires retraining of the neuromuscular complex (muscles, tendons, ligaments, and peripheral nervous system) to respond appropriately and adequately to outside forces acting on the body in a way that prevents further irritation or injury. For example, inversion of a recently injured ankle on the edge of a sidewalk might result in reinjury or worsening of the injury without appropriate proprioceptive feedback and response. Therefore, rehabilitation means retraining injured structures and additional muscles and tendon structures that could develop inherent forces to respond quickly to outside forces in order to prevent injury.

Training surfaces may also affect injury recurrences. Hard surfaces (i.e., concrete) result in more deceleration forces on the lower body. Uphill or soft (sand) running surfaces cause increased stretching of the posterior lower leg, while downhill running causes increased deceleration forces to be applied to the anterior lower leg and knee. Running laps in one direction continuously on an oval track requires the inner leg stride to be shorter than that of the outer leg, and therefore different forces act on each leg. Running on banked or uneven sidewalks causes a relative leg length discrepancy and may cause problems with the iliotibial band or knee and hip irritation.

Foremost in these preventative measures is the education of the exercise participant in terms of cause, rehabilitation, and prevention of injuries. If the participants understand the forces that can cause or aggravate the injury, they may be more able to prevent recurrences and be more willing to participate in rehabilitation.

Sports and exercise involve the application of forces by the participant against outside forces from the environment or other athletes, and the control of this biomechanical interaction for increased competition skills, health, and enjoyment. It is important that sports medicine and health care personnel understand these forces for appropriate and timely care of the sports injury.

Chapter 3

Basic Mechanics of Biological Tissues

A basic understanding of the biomechanics of the biological tissues involved in the human musculoskeletal system is necessary before discussing the prevention of injuries. Knowing the basic structure and function of these tissues will provide us with insight to the loads and stresses which are placed on the body during high level activity. Additionally, knowledge of tissue mechanics allows us to understand the repairing capabilities of the structures.

The biological tissues under consideration in this chapter are bone, cartilage, ligament, tendon, muscle, and skin. From a biomechanical standpoint, bones are the transmitters of the forces produced by the muscle; thereby, causing movement to occur. They accomplish this by a system of machines (i.e. lever, pulley, wheel-axle). Cartilage functions to serve as a reducer of friction between bony surfaces and to distribute loads across the joints. Ligaments hold bones together. Tendons serve as muscle attachments to bone. Skin gives protection to the underlying structures of the body.

Properties of Biological Tissue

Two mechanical properties are associated with biological tissues: strength and stiffness. The strength of the tissue depends upon the rate of loading (stress), the direction of loading, and muscle activity. Stiffness, on the other hand, depends upon the resistance to deformation when a load is applied. To understand what happens when a load is applied in a given direction, one can construct a load-deformation curve (Nordin & Frankel, 1989). (See Fig. 3.1)

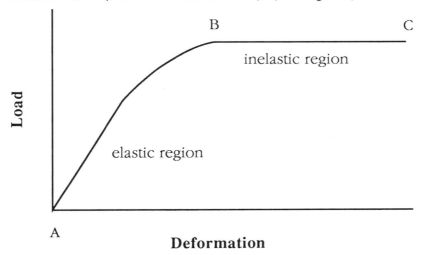

Figure 3.1.
Load-deformation curve. (Adapted with permission from Nordin and Frankel, 1989.)

A biological tissue has the ability to be deformed and then returned to its original shape and condition. The amount of deformation and the ability to be restored to the original state depends upon the loading. In Fig. 3.1, the elastic region (A-B) represents the region where a load, if released, does not cause any permanent deformation or residual damage. If loading continues, there comes a point at which some permanent deformation will result (B-C), and perhaps a point at which the tissue fails completely (C). An example of normal elastic flexibility is a joint stretching out to its normal range of motion. Joints stretched beyond normal to subluxation or dislocation are forced into the plastic region and damage occurs.

The area under the curve represents the amount of energy which can be stored before failure. Under rapid loading conditions, large amounts of energy are stored. If loading continues to the point of failure, the energy stored is released which usually results in a more severe injury. If loading conditions are slow in nature, the energy stored can be dissipated. This results in a less severe injury.

The slope of the line in the elastic region indicates the stiffness of the material. A value can be assigned to the amount of stiffness. This is called *Young's modulus of elasticity*. The value is obtained by dividing the stress at any point in the elastic portion of the curve by the strain at that point.

In general, loads that are applied more rapidly cause stiffer bone performance. The term viscoelastic is used to associate the changes in tissue in relation to load over time. The stiffer the material is, the less viscoelastic. However, even metal rods are given some viscoelastic factor. The order of viscoelasticity of materials predictably is skin, cartilage, tendon, bone and metal. Bone is approximately 10 to 20 times more viscoelastic than is stainless steel. (Cochran, 1982)

The load per unit area (stress) and the amount/percent of deformation (strain) can be determined using samples of standardized shape and size. This is what enables us to compare different materials. A stress-strain curve is thus generated. The appearance of the stress-strain curve is very much like the load-deformation curve. A comparison of the stress-strain curves for metal, glass, bone is shown in Fig. 3.2.

Metal is a material which has the capability of absorbing large amounts of energy before failure (ductility) as indicated by the long plastic region. Glass, on the other hand, has little capability of absorbing large amounts of energy before failure (brittleness). This is indicated by a lack of any plastic region. Bone is not linearly elastic. That is, some yielding may occur when the bone is loaded in the elastic region.

It is important to note that collagenous tissue placed under normal stress in the elastic region will recover in a pattern similar to the way it reacted when the load was applied. That is, as a tension load is first applied, there is an initial

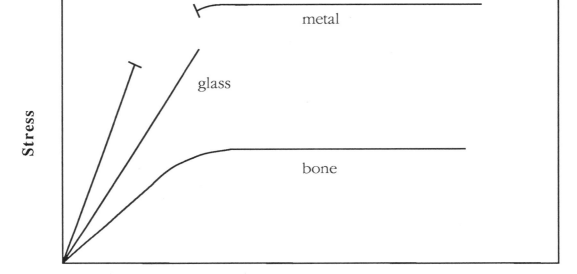

Figure 3.2.
Stress-strain curve. (Adapted with permission from Nordin and Frankel, 1989)

large magnitude change in length, followed by a slower rise to a plateau. As the load is removed, there initially is a large magnitude of recovery, followed by a slower drop to the normal length. Although this is true of all collagenous tissues including bone, there are significant individual differences between the tissues which require attention.

Bone Mechanics

The function of bone is not only to transmit the forces produced by the muscles, but also to serve as the support system for the body, the protector of vital organs, the site for the production of red blood cells, and the site for storage of calcium and other minerals. It is susceptible to high stresses, but fortunately for us, it is highly adaptable to the stresses and constantly undergoes remodeling. To fully understand how bone reacts to an injury and how it repairs itself, it is necessary to understand its basic structure and composition, and how it behaves under loading/stress.

Bone Structure

Bone structure is either cortical or trabecular. Cortical bone, also known as compact bone, has a dense texture and is stiff. Trabecular bone, also known as cancellous bone, has a spongy texture and is not very stiff.

The differences between cortical and trabecular bone are summarized in Table 3.1.

Table 3.1 Differences Between Cortical and Trabecular Bone.

Cortical	Trabecular
5-30% porous	30-90% porous
withstands greater stress, but less strain before failure	high energy storage capability
not easily deformed	easily deformed

As aging occurs, trabecular bone becomes thinner or is resorbed. This is why old bone cannot withstand as much strain as young bone. A more in-depth explanation may be found in Ch. 6 where aging-related injuries and their prevention are discussed.

Bone Tissue Composition

Bone tissue is made up of organic (30%) and inorganic (70%) material. The remaining organic material consists of noncollagenous proteins and cells (osteoblasts, osteocytes, osteoclasts). Collagen, a fibrous insoluble protein, is by far the most abundant of the organic material found in bone. It gives bone its elasticity, and responds well to high tensile stresses. It, however, does not respond well to high compressive stresses. Collagen stores may be reduced because of a lack of activity. On the other hand, exercise increases the amount found in the bone tissues. Bone material which is lacking protein will be very brittle and fracture easily. Conversely, bone which is de-mineralized will be flexible, but cannot withstand compressive forces. Generally, young school children have a higher ratio of protein to mineral content in their softer bones. They, therefore, sustain more "greenstick" types of fractures than elderly populations. The inverse is true of older people who have more brittle bones which fracture more easily. (Kaplan, 1987)

The inorganic, or mineral component of bone, consists mainly of hydroxyapatites. This is a basic calcium phosphate in which the calcium ions are surrounded by phosphate and hydroxyl ions. This gives stiffness and hardness to bones. It can be stored in either cortical or trabecular bone. It is highly resistant to compressive stresses, but not to tensile stresses. (Kaplan, 1987)

Bone Formation

The formation of bone tissue begins in utero and continues into the second decade of life. Bones may be formed by intramembranous ossification or endochondral ossification. Those bones which serve protective functions such as the flat bone (e.g. skull, sternum), short bones (e.g. tarsals, carpals), and irregular bones (e.g. vertebrae) form by intramembranous ossification. The long bones (e.g. femur, humerus) of the body form by endochondral ossification. That is, there is an intervening cartilage model. The cartilage is separated from the ossified bone by an epiphyseal plate. (See Fig. 3.3) Growth continues until the bone is ossified and the epiphyseal plate has closed. The epiphysis and epiphyseal plate have been implicated in youth sport injuries, and will be discussed further in Ch. 6.

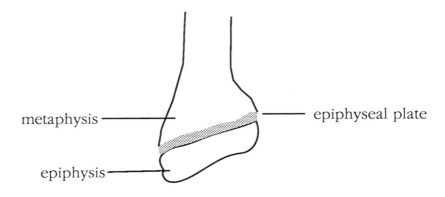

Figure 3.3.
Epiphyseal plate.

Bone Remodeling

Bone constantly undergoes remodeling. It changes its shape and adjusts its mass. Mineral stores and collagen are redistributed. Structure is changed by an alteration in the amounts of cortical and trabecular bone. These changes may be due to mechanical stresses, inactivity, nutrition, or disease. Remodeling occurs according to Wolff's Law which states that "Bone is laid down where needed and resorbed where not needed."

Bone Behavior Under Loading

Bone behaves differently depending upon the type of stress placed upon it. The five stresses discussed here will be tensile, compressive, shearing, torsional, and bending. (Nordin & Frankel, 1989)

Tension. Tensile stresses (See definitions, Ch. 1) pull in opposite directions at the end of a bone. An example of a tensile force is the strong contraction of the gastrocnemius and soleus muscles pulling on the calcaneus at its attachment via the Achilles' tendon. A great enough force may cause a rupture of the tendon or even a tensile fracture through the calcaneus.

Compression. Compressive stresses (See definitions, Ch.1) cause a "crushing" sensation, or stresses from opposite ends of a bone being directed toward each other. Jumping from a height and landing on the feet causes a compressive stress in the vertebrae.

Shear. Shearing stresses (See definitions, Ch.1) cause two ends of a bone to move in opposite and parallel directions to each other. For example, the epiphyseal plate may be sheared away from the ossified bone in a young child when hit on the outside of the knee (valgus stress) while the foot is planted.

Torsion. Torsional stresses (See definitions, Ch. 1) cause a twisting action around the axis of the bone. A skier who has lost his/her balance and whose ski bindings have not released properly may experience a twisting of the lower leg resulting in a tibial spiral fracture.

Bending.   Bending stresses cause both tensile and compressive stresses on a bone. If a skier were to fall forward over his/her boots, tensile stresses would be placed on the posterior side of the leg, while the anterior portion of the leg would experience compressive stresses. In order of strongest to weakest, bone withstands compression best. This is followed by tension and shear forces. This fact would seem to fit well in our gravity dominated environment.

Articular Cartilage Mechanics

Articular cartilage reacts to loads somewhat like a waterbed. Cartilage is 60-80% water, and its resulting stiffness and deformation depends greatly on the load per unit area and the time over which the load is applied. Some old style waterbeds were like sleeping on top of a water balloon with very little substructure to stiffen them. With the addition of baffles and foam cells, much like the fibrous substructure of cartilage, waterbeds are now firmer.

Cartilage also is a dynamic structure in comparison to other connective tissue because there is a resultant flow of water in and out of it depending on the amount of pressure and length of time it is applied. Loads applied suddenly do not allow time for water to flow out, and therefore, cartilage reacts like elastic and recovers its original shape quickly. For example, if one were to depress quickly a water-filled sponge, the sponge would be restored to its original position without having lost any, or little, of the water. On the other hand, if the sponge was depressed slowly, it would be restored to its original position, but would have lost some of its water. An example of this may be illustrated in the cartilage during standing and sitting. Loads applied continuously such as in long term standing, cause some deformation as the water has time to be pressed out of the tissue. Likewise, on the release of the pressure, when you sit down, the cartilage will return to normal shape, but not instantaneously as it did under the sudden load condition. Cartilage is very viscoelastic and therefore, the stress/strain curve is dependent on the rate of loading. (See Figure 3.4)

Another biomechanical consideration of cartilage is that it is both self lubricating and wear resistant. That is, under normal use, the pumping action on the cells stimulate the joint to lubricate itself as well as to heal any damage done by the compression. It also is true that the greater the joint range of excursion, the greater the surface area contact. This reduces the "focused" shear force and frictional wear on the cartilage surface. For example, there is the potential for greater knee articular surface damage due to wear from long, slow distance

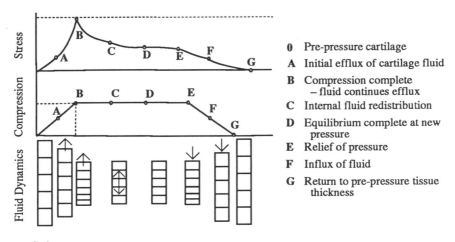

Figure 3.4.

Cartilage stress, compression and fluid dynamics. (Adapted from *Injury and Repair of the Musculoskeletal Soft Tissues;* Woo, Sl-Y & Buckwalter, J. A. [Eds.]: 1988, Park Ridge, IL: American Academy of Orthopedic Surgeons.)

The diagram legend reads:

0 Pre-pressure cartilage
A Initial efflux of cartilage fluid
B Compression complete – fluid continues efflux
C Internal fluid redistribution
D Equilibrium complete at new pressure
E Relief of pressure
F Influx of fluid
G Return to pre-pressure tissue thickness

running, than from playing basketball, where the knee goes through greater ranges of motion. Of course, the basketball player has higher risks of damaging the knee in other ways besides frictional wear.

Ligament and Tendon Mechanics

The composition of ligaments and tendons is very similar. They consist primarily of two components: collagen and elastin. Collagen provides strength and stiffness to the tissues, while elastin provides extensibility. A third component, ground substance, is a friction reducing gelatinous solution between fibers.

Basic Structure of Ligaments and Tendons

The collagen fibers are oriented parallel to each other and in line with the direction of normal functional forces. Collagen dominates the mass of the structure (70% of its dry weight). (Curwin & Standish, 1984) It is a combination of amino acids which form into triple helix formations called tropocollagen. These tropocollagen cells overlap each other, usually in groups of five, and thus, form the microfibriles.

Microfibriles further organize into subfibriles, fibriles, fascicle, and finally the tendon or ligament. They appear glossy white or pearl in color.

The fiber orientation of collagenous tissue varies considerably with the type and function. Generally, tendon has the most regular and parallel formation of fibers, followed by the ligaments of major joints such as the anterior and posterior cruciate ligaments of the knee. The fibers continue to be less parallel when considering joint capsule and fascia, and the skin has the most diverse and least regular organization of collagen fiber (Cochran, 1982). (See Figure 3.5.) The variations in fiber orientation are directly related to the types of stresses that each structure is expected to endure. Chapter 4 gives more information on this functional principle.

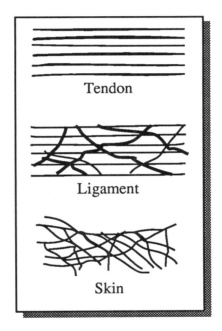

Figure 3.5.
Collagen Fiber. Orientation in tendon, ligament and skin.

The metabolism of tendons and ligaments is slow, although not non-existent or inert as once thought. Studies have reported that the turnover rate for muscle was 50 days, liver 30 days, and collagen requires 50-100 days. Ligaments primarily get their blood supply from periarticular arterial plexuses. Tendons get some circulation from the musculotendinous junction and the tendon-bone junction. The ligament-bone insertion sites are, however, nearly avascular and those vessels present are easily damaged. (Curwin & Standish, 1984)

The fibers of the tendon and ligament are wavy and "crimped" in appearance under microscopic inspection. When a load is applied, these waves straighten out and are responsible for the stretch capacity of the structure. Collagen fibers begin to fail or break at 6-8% increase in length, whereas, elastin has a greater capacity to stretch (approximately 2x the original length) before damage. Once elastin has extended to its limit, it becomes brittle and breaks. The elastin fibers are responsible for the reorientation of the collagen fibers into wavy configurations after the load is released. (See Figure 3.6)

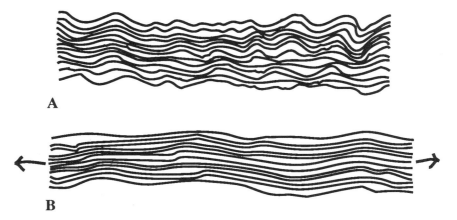

Figure 3.6.
Ligament collagen fiber function. A) Relaxed "crimped" appearance of ligament collagen fibers. B) Less collagen fiber undulation or crimped appearance under tensile strain.

Ligament and Tendon Fiber Ratios

Individual ligaments display more variable ratios of collagen to elastin than do tendons, depending on their individual function. The more specific the direction of stress on the ligament, the higher the collagen content. If the ligament is required to have strength in several directions, the elastin content is higher. For instance, the anterior cruciate ligament which primarily handles tensile loads has a very high collagen content (90%); whereas, the ligamentum flavum of the spine has a higher content of elastin (60-70%). Tendons have more regular component ratios, all being high in collagen due to their more exclusive tensile functions.

Muscle Mechanics

Muscle tissue consists of four major parts: (1) muscle fibers, (2) connective tissue, (3) blood vessels, and (4) nerves. (Spielholz, 1982) For the purpose of understanding the biomechanics of muscle, we will concentrate on the muscle fiber and connective tissue here.

Muscles have the unique property of producing forces. The forces are produced within the body and act on other body parts. They also may act or react to the external environment.

Components of Muscle Tissue

The basic component of muscle tissue is the muscle fiber, which is made up of several hundred to several thousand myofibrils. Each myofibril is composed of the two protein filaments responsible for muscle contraction, actin and myosin. The actin and myosin filaments are organized into units called sarcomeres with a surrounding sarcoplasmic reticulum.

These overlapping protein filaments, actin and myosin, are central to the contraction process as actin is chemically attracted to active sites of myosin and slide along the myosin filament causing a shortening of the myofibril. Of course, several thousand shortening myofibrils within one muscle fiber, and several hundred fibers also shortening in unison, create the shortening of the total muscle. (See Figure 3.7)

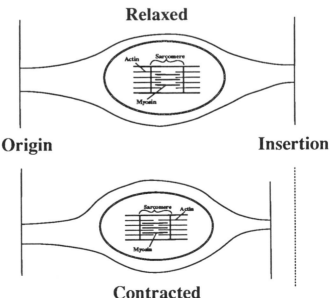

Figure 3.7.
Muscle Contraction Diagram.

Muscle Contraction

The initiation of the contraction process is caused by the nerve stimulus to the muscle (action potential). In brief, the action potential spreads electro/chemical current through to the calcium ions in the myofibrils and as the concentration in calcium ions increases, they flow into the area of the actin and myosin filaments causing the contraction. The forces caused by the contraction of the muscle are harnessed by the connective tissue (sarcoplasmic reticulum) surrounding the myofibrils. Collagen and elastin fibers are derived from the sarcoplasmic reticulum. As the hierarchy of connective tissue progresses, they form the tendon at the end of the muscle.

Biomechanically, muscle tissue is very dynamic with the capacity to contract in two functional ways: (1) isometric, and (2) isotonic. Isotonic contractions are further divided into concentric (shortening), and eccentric (lengthening) contractions. (See definitions, Ch. 1.)

Passive/Elastic Qualities of Muscle

In addition to their active capabilities, muscles also have passive qualities during the relaxed state which contribute to normal movement. The passive functions of muscle, in biomechanical terms, are tone and elasticity. For example, EMG studies have shown that there is passive elastic hip extension during normal walking gait which is responsible for 60 to 100 per cent of the motion. (Deusinger, 1984) Muscle tone can be described as the natural resistance to motion that is present in a relaxed muscle. Muscle tone is very important, as anyone who has observed either a denervated muscle in a totally flaccid state, or excessive tone to the point of spasticity, can tell you. A clinical example of a low tone condition is a brachial plexus (peripheral) nerve injury. High tone conditions usually come from central nervous system lesions such as cerebral palsy, head injury, or spinal cord injury.

Skin Mechanics
Basic Skin Structure

The structural components of skin are keratin, collagen and elastin. The arrangement of collagen fibers in skin is more diffuse and disorganized than any other connective tissue. But even with this relative disorganization of mechanical strength, there are areas where the collagen fibers are oriented more in one direction than another. These lines of collagenous orientation are called Langer lines, and they vary greatly in their orientation on different parts of the body. That is, they are generally perpendicular to the spine; however, across joints of limbs they may be either perpendicular or parallel depending on the specific joint and the flexor or extensor surface. For example, the elbow has Langer lines parallel to the limb on the flexion side and perpendicular on the extensor side.

Skin Strength and Mechanical Properties

The strength of animal skin has been tested and was found to be stronger in parallel to the collagen fibers. A skin laceration occurs more often parallel to than perpendicular to these lines of collagen fibers. (Haut, 1985) This may sound paradoxical, but it follows that skin would break more easily along the lines of strength, just as wood splits in the direction of the grain as opposed to across the grain. (See Figure 3.8)

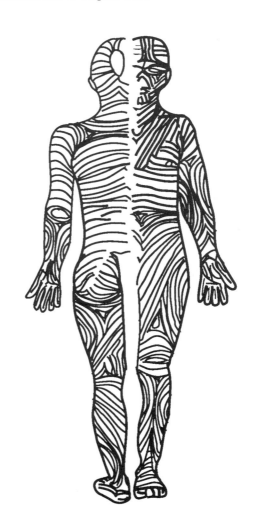

Figure 3.8.
Langer's lines, subcutaneous fibrous connective tissue.

The mechanical properties of skin also are influenced by its attachment to the underlying fascia, and the fact that it is continuously attached to the rest of the skin of the body. All of these properties, and other insulating factors not covered here, make the skin a marvelous connective tissue which covers the body and protects it from internal and external forces, as well as helping to control body temperature and defend against infection and disease.

Summary

A knowledge of the anatomy and biomechanical function of bone, articular cartilage, ligament, tendon, muscle, and skin aids in the understanding of why injuries occur. Biological tissue has the capability of being deformed and then restored to its normal shape and condition. When stresses are placed on the tissues, permanent deformation may or may not occur. Permanent deformation usually indicates damage to the tissue. This information is valuable in knowing how to prevent injuries.

Review Questions

1. What functions do bones, muscles, ligaments, tendons, and skin serve in the body?

2. Distinguish between strength and stiffness of a biological tissue.

3. Refer to the load-deformation curve and describe the implications for loads released in the elastic region? in the inelastic region?

4. Define Young's modulus of elasticity.

5. What is the most viscoelastic of the biological tissues? the least viscoelastic?

6. Distinguish between cortical and trabecular bone.

7. What is the most abundant source of organic material in bone? What is its function?

8. Describe what happens to bone tissue composition with aging.

9. Describe Wolff's Law in regard to bone remodeling.

10. Define and give an example of the five stresses which may be placed on a bone.

11. How does cartilage react to loading under rapid loading? slow loading?

12. How is wear and tear on cartilage surfaces avoided?

13. What are the four basic components of ligament and tendon tissue?

14. Describe the difference in collagen fiber orientation between tendon, ligament, and skin.

15. At what amount of elongation do collagen fibers normally begin to break?

16. At what amount of elongation do elastin fibers normally begin to break?

17. Explain the terms "plastic" and "elastic" in relation to tissue strain.

18. In general, do tendons or ligaments have higher ratio of collagen to elastin, and why?

19. Name the two basic proteins that are responsible for muscle function.

20. What is the term for the connective tissue supporting muscle tissue that forms into tendon at the end of the muscle?

21. What are two possible functions of muscle tissue?

22. Explain the functions of Langer lines in skin.

23. In general, explain the variances in skin strength in relation to its direction on the body.

References

Cochran, G. V. B. (1982). <u>A Primer of Orthopedic Biomechanics</u>. New York, NY: Churchill Livingstons Inc.

Cornwell, M. (1984). Biomechanics of noncontractile tissue. <u>Physical Therapy</u>, <u>64</u>(12):1869-1873.

Curwin, S., & Standish, W. (1984). <u>Tendonitis: Its Etiology and Treatment</u>. Lexington: D. C. Heath and Co.

Deusinger, R. H. (1984, December). Biomechanics in clinical practice. <u>Physical Therapy, 64</u>(12):1860-1868.

Haut, R. C. (1985). Studies on the rate sensitive failure characteristics of skin in tension. In D. Butler, T. K. Hung, & R. E. Mates (Eds.), <u>1985 Biomechanics Symposium</u>.

Kaplan, F. S. (1987). Osteoporosis: Pathophysiology and prevention. <u>Clinical Symposia</u>, <u>39</u>(1):1-32.

Nicholas, J. A., & Hershman, E. B. (1986). <u>The Lower Extremity and Spine in Sports Medicine</u>. St. Louis: C. V. Mosby Co.

Nordin, M. & Frankel, V. H. (1989). <u>Basic Biomechanics of the Skeletal System</u>. Philadelphia, PA: Lea and Febiger.

Spielholz, N. I. (1982, December). Skeletal muscle: A review of its development in vivo and in vitro. <u>Physical Therapy</u>, <u>62</u>(12):1757-1762.

Wainwright, S. A. (1986). Fibrous skin mechanics: Suprastructure and new problems. In G. W. Schmid-Schönbein, S. L.-Y. Woo, & B. W. Zweifoch (Eds.), <u>Frontiers in Biomechanics</u>. New York: Springer Verlag.

Chapter 4

Mechanisms of Tissue Injury

To understand how and why an injury happens, there are several questions that must be answered. Three of the most important questions are listed below.

1. What specific tissue is injured?

2. What is the source of the injury causing force?

3. What are the biomechanical characteristics of that tissue?

Chapter 3 more directly answers question 3 above and questions 1 and 2 will be considered here. The answers to these questions can potentially prevent the injury from happening or prevent it from recurring in someone who has already experienced an injury.

Knowing which tissue is injured is not always easy unless it is visible such as the skin. It is the task of the evaluation and diagnosis process that is performed by doctors, physical therapists, and athletic trainers to make this determination within their scope of practice. Their training in anatomy, function, and bio-mechanics of the body, together with an accurate history of the injury, will lead them to the specific tissue or tissues involved. More often than not, there are multiple tissues injured to various degrees. For example, the common second degree ankle ligament sprain may also strain the peroneal muscles on the lateral leg, while contusing the medial tarsal bones of the foot as they approximate with the medial malleolus. These injuries are in addition to the anterior talo fibular ligament and joint capsule sprain.

Once the specific tissues are determined, the characteristics of these tissues' biomechanical strength and function are considered. In Chapter 2 the anatomical structures which are commonly injured in sports activities were described. To follow-up on that information, an explanation will be given here concerning how that tissue responds to the variety of forces that are experienced during activity. For the purpose of having even greater understanding of the forces on these tissues, they are divided further into two classifications of 1) active, and 2) passive forces.

Active and Passive Forces

Active forces are defined as forces that originate in the body, or muscular forces. These forces are either isotonic (concentric or eccentric), or isometric. For the purposes of this discussion we will say that all active forces come from within the body.

Passive forces may be from either inside the body, such as limb weight (affected by gravity), or from outside the body such as another player, wind; or water resistance. Below are some examples of a few active and passive forces. You will no doubt notice that the list of passive forces has the potential to be longer and more varied than the active force list.

Active Forces

a. Pectoral muscles during bench press
b. Hamstring muscles during swing phase of gait
c. Extensor carpi radialis during backhand in tennis
d. Hip extensors during blocking in football
e. Abdominal muscle contraction after the pole plant in pole vault

Passive Forces

a. Centrifugal force during throwing motion
b. Buoyancy during swimming
c. Gravity in weight lifting
d. Wind resistance during cycling
e. Momentum of football players as they collide
f. Ground reaction force at heel strike in running
g. Friction between skin and shoe

The critical consideration may be the athlete's or participant's preparation and training for the activity. Elements of both active and passive forces are usually involved in the injury, just as they are in normal function. The astute practitioner may be able to determine whether an injury, or failure of a tissue, was due to primarily active or passive forces and take preventative measures. For example, a distance runner has patello-femoral pain from excessive patellar compression. The evaluation reveals that the problem is not from her shoes, training habits, or biomechanics of running style, but weak lower quadriceps muscles which do not adequately stabilize the patella. Excessive friction is produced causing the irritation. Work on the active component of strengthening would be indicated. An example of a passive force is a hit to the head in football causing hyperextension of the neck and the pinch of a nerve (stinger). This problem could be addressed by both strengthening the neck and wearing a neck roll for prevention of hyperextension.

Injury Force

The question of where the injury causing force originated is certainly worth some thought, and we will investigate that now. If there is an intent to prevent injury, this question requires an answer. We already have been introduced to active and passive forces. Active forces are applied by the participant's own muscle, and passive processes are basically all others.

To prevent active force injuries, there are two primary concerns: 1) having adequate functional strength, and 2) having adequate balance of strength. Admittedly, these two points are almost the same, however; the second point is so often overlooked that its distinction is warranted.

Since the late 1960's, resistance training has become a regular part of organized competitive athletics. At first it was just football players, wrestlers, and track and field weight men and women who subjected themselves to the rigors of the weight room. Now resistance training is used in almost all sports and at all age levels. Many of the improvements in performance have been directly attributed to hard work and dedication to a resistance program which increases the active force the participant can produce. The danger now is that the participant who does not have adequate strength preparation will not only do poorly competitively, but particularly in the case of contact sports, be subjecting him or herself to injury.

The reason the adjective "functional" is included in the statement "having adequate functional strength" is that resistance training is not always functional for the sport or activity. Coaches, teachers and medical personnel are realizing that specificity of training is of utmost importance. For instance, consider a squat exercise with a weight machine involving hips and knees moving through the range of motion at 60° per second. This exercise does stimulate common motion in sports. However, it does not match the functional speed required to fire out and block an opposing lineman or accomplish a jump maneuver as in basketball (exceeding 200° per second at the knee).

Another functional specificity problem related to resistance training is matching the biomechanical position of the body. One prime example of this problem is to review the popular knee extension machine. The participant is seated with the trunk, hip and knee at 90° with the foot free or in an open chain position. How many sports depend on strength in this position? Perhaps when you boot a couch pillow at the T.V.!

The importance of maintaining a balance of strength has been appreciated for several years. Hamstring to quadriceps ratios, biceps to triceps, and abdominal to low back extensors, are a few examples. For the person who casually trains with weights, and does not have the benefit of a coach, it is tempting to "do what he/she does best." This encourages muscle strength imbalance as the weaker antagonist is ignored. One simple, but not always practical, answer to this problem is to initially strength test the athlete and require him or her to only work on the weaker component until the balance is restored. Below is a table of strength ratios for common areas of the body.

Table 4.1 Strength Ratio Percentages

Reciprocal strength ratio normative data for males and females. Adapted from J. G. Davies, et al. (1980). A Descriptive Muscular Strength and Power Analysis of the U.S. Cross Country Ski Team (Abstract), *Medicine and Science in Sports and Exercise, 12* (2), 441.

Movement	Males	Females
Elbow Flexion/Extension 45°/sec	70	65
Shoulder Flexion / Extension 45°/sec	60	48
Shoulder Abduction/ Adduction 60°/sec	66	53
Hip Flexion/Ext 45°/sec	66	64
Knee Flex/Ext * 45°/sec	61	57
Ankle Plantar flex/dorsi flex 45°/sec	26	24

* Author recommends higher ratio of Knee Flex/Ext to prevent patella femoral problems or in cases of knee ligament instability.

Injury Description and Causes

The human body endures many different types of injuries from a variety of forces. Below is a list and explanation of the most common types.

1. **Abrasion** — a disruption of the skin to include both the dermis and epidermis. The cause is usually a shear force as the skin scrapes across a surface which tears away a layer of skin to expose blood capillaries. Example: A track athlete hits a hurdle and falls to the track scraping the skin of the knees and palms.

2. **Contusion** — an injury to underlying tissue such as muscle, fascia or periosteum. The force is usually from a blunt hard contact which is sufficient to disrupt blood vessels and cause an accumulation of blood in the tissue. Example: A basketball player is driving for a layup and his thigh collides with the defender's knee.

3. **Laceration** — a cut or tear in the skin having rough edges. The force is usually caused by a sharp and/or hard object coming in contact with the body. Lacerations are more common where the underlying muscle or fat layer is thin and does not provide as much cushion, such as about the face or head. Example: A wrestler is butted in the head and sustains an injury to the supra orbital area.

4. **Strain** — an elongation of muscle or tendon beyond the elastic limit where actual tearing or breaking of some fibers is present. Strains are caused by excessive tensile forces which result in a few, several, or in the case of a complete rupture, all the fibers to break. Example: A softball player is attempting to run out a ground ball and as he reaches for first base, he overstretches the hamstring.

5. **Sprain** — the stretching and tearing of ligaments or capsular (non-contractile) tissue. The causative force may be tensile, shear or rotary in direction, with enough magnitude to force the tissue beyond the elastic region and to failure of a few, some, or all the fibers. Example: A soccer goalie gets hit on the thumb by a hard driving goal shot which bends the thumb back, hyperextending the metacarpal phalangeal joint.

6. **Fracture** — the disruption of the normal matrix of bone tissue. The severity may vary from a small "hairline" crack in the cortex such as a stress fracture, to complete fragmentation of bone material with some fragments puncturing the skin. Forces commonly causing fractures are shear, compressions or torsional. Another type of fracture force may be tensile. An avulsion fracture is where the insertion of a ligament or tendon pulls away from the bone. The specific type of fracture producing force may be determined by an x-ray which reveals the specific type and extent of the fracture. Example: A lacrosse player falls laterally on his shoulder sustaining compression of the clavicle, and resultant fracture.

7. **Puncture** — a small break in the skin from a pointed object. The injury causing force is usually perpendicular to the skin and focused on a small area, making the force per unit area overcome the strength of the skin. Example: A track athlete who has fallen on the track is run over by an oncoming runner who is wearing spikes.

8. **Subluxation** — an injury to a joint which is forced beyond its normal limit of motion between the two articulating bones. It is sometimes called a partial dislocation. The responsible force may be tensile or compressive, and usually involves some shear and/or torsional force. The initial injury force is usually from an external or passive origin, but after the joint capsule and supportive ligaments have been sprained and loosened, active muscle force may be enough to sublux a joint. Example: A rugby player gets hit in the anterior-medial aspect of the knee, pushing the patella laterally.

9. **Dislocation** — a severe joint injury where the articulating bones completely lose their alignment with each other and are non-functional. Another term which represents the same degree of joint injury is luxation. The forces responsible for a dislocation are the same as for subluxation above, except the magnitude of the force is greater and sufficient enough to cause the loss of joint integrity.

   There is usually significant soft tissue or supportive structure damage as ligaments and joint capsules sprain or rupture, and/or cartilage is torn. Example: A baseball catcher gets hit on the fingers of the throwing hand while catching the ball. The impact pushes a finger joint completely out of alignment.

10. **Inflammation** — an irritation and swelling of tissue causing pain and additional friction. The force causing the inflammation is usually a repeated micro-trauma from excessive tensile strain for muscles and tendons, and shear and compressive forces for joints. The suffix "itis" indicates the presence of inflammation as in the terms tendonitis, myositis, arthritis and capsulitis. Example: A tennis player consistently hits the backhand shot with too much wrist motion and develops lateral elbow pain.

Summary

The person trying to determine the injury causing force has an interesting and challenging task. Detailed descriptions of the incident of injury by the participant or athlete, or other eye witness reports are very important. Often in organized competition sports there are films of the incident which can be reviewed. Sports medicine personnel are to beware of judging injuries too quickly without a thorough evaluation. What may appear to be a simple sprain, may in fact be an avulsion or fracture. The investigation of the mechanism of injury is part of the prevention process as the participant gets appropriate treatment for his/her problems. And then, through an understanding of the mechanism of injury, the participant has a chance to prevent it from recurring.

Review Questions

1. Explain the difference between active and passive forces, and give some examples.

2. Discuss the problems with resistance training and specificity for functional sport participation.

3. Explain the difference between an abrasion and a laceration, and the forces involved.

4. What specific force is usually responsible for strain injuries in muscle or tendon?

114149

5. Explain the difference between a sprain and strain and give examples.

6. Describe the force causing avulsion fractions.

7. Explain the difference between a subluxation and a dislocation.

8. What is the causing force of most inflammatory injuries?

References

Arnheim, D. D. (1985). Modern Principals of Athletic Training. St. Louis: Times Mirror/Mosby College Company.

Cochran, G. V. B. (1982). A Primer of Orthopedic Biomechanics. New York, NY: Churchill Livingstons Inc.

Nordin, M. (1980). Biomechanics of collagenous tissue. In V. H. Frankel, & M. Nordin (Eds.), Basic Biomechanics of the Skeletal System (pp. 87-110). Philadelphia, PA: Lea and Febiger.

Rodgers, M. M., & Cavanaugh, P. R. (1984). Glossary of biomechanical terms, concepts, and units. Physical Therapy, 64(12):1886-1902.

Suggested Readings

Cornwell, M. (1984). Biomechanics of noncontractile tissue. Physical Therapy, 64(12).

Curwin, S., & Standish, W. (1984). Tendonitis: Its Etiology and Treatment. Lexington: D. C. Heath and Co.

Krejci, V., & Koch, P. (1979). <u>Muscle and Tendon Injuries in Athletes</u>. Chicago: G. Thieme Publishers.

Westcott, W. L. (1982). <u>Strength Fitness</u>. Boston: Allyn and Bacon, Inc.

Yamada, H. (1970). In G. F. Evans (Ed.), <u>Strength of Biological Materials</u>. Baltimore: Williams and Wilkins.

Chapter 5

Interrelationship of Injury and Anatomical Structure and Function

Cranium and Brain Coverings
 Structure and Function
 Mechanisms of Head Injury
 Common Head Injuries

Mandible and Maxilla
 Structure and Function
 Mechanisms of Injury
 Mandible-Maxilla Injuries

Nose, Eyes, Ears, Teeth
 Nose
 Eyes
 Ears
 Teeth

The Spine
 Structure and Function
 Mechanisms of Injury
 Common Spinal Column Injuries and Impairments

Thorax

The Shoulder
 Structure and Function
 Mechanisms of Injury
 Common Shoulder Injuries

The Arm and Elbow
 Structure and Function
 Common Arm and Elbow Injuries

The human skeleton is a machine composed of a system of levers, pulleys, and wheel-axles. It is propelled by the contraction of the muscles which surround the bones and joints. The location of the muscle attachments in relation to the joint axis dictates the movement efficiency of this system. (See Chapter 1 for definition of levers.) Generally speaking, the human body is composed of Class III levers. This gives it the advantage of speed and range of movement at the sacrifice of moving a heavy load with minimal effort. In terms of machines, this is not the most efficient design. Additionally, the optimum angle at which a muscle must pull to move the levers cannot always be achieved.

Another important factor regarding the structure and function of the human skeletal system is the external force of gravity which constantly acts on the system. To add to the problem, the skeletal structure is not ideally suited for the upright stance characteristic of bipeds.

However, for all of the "machine design" flaws, there are some structural and functional advantages for the human body. These make it possible for the body to adapt quite well to the environment in which it lives.

It is the purpose of this chapter to examine the structure and function of the basic segments and joints of the body. An understanding of how the system is designed to function can lead to a better understanding of how injuries occur and what needs to be done to prevent them from occurring.

Cranium and Brain Coverings

The scalp, skull (consisting of the cranium and facial bones), and brain are involved in some of the most devastating kinds of injuries. Permanent neurological deficiences can sometimes occur as a result of the impact/collision situations involving the head.

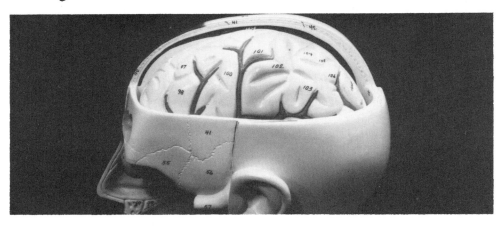

Figure 5.1. Scalp, skull, brain model.

Structure and Function

The scalp is a 5-layered structure consisting of:

S   skin which contains the hair follicles
C   connective tissue which contains blood vessels
A   aponeurosis epicranialis which acts as a "helmet" over the crainum
L   loose connective tissue which intervenes between the "helmet" and the cranial covering
P   pericranium which covers the skull

The first three layers act as one, and often remain as a unit when a severe laceration occurs. The aponeurosis and epicranialis muscle are strong structures which protect the scalp from further gaping. The subaponeurotic layer (loose connective tissue) contains many spaces which are capable of filling with fluid. It is considered to be a dangerous area, and is susceptible to the spread of infection via the emissary veins.

The function of the cranium is to support and protect the brain. One of the ways it does this is via configuration of its internal compartments. (See Fig. 5.2)

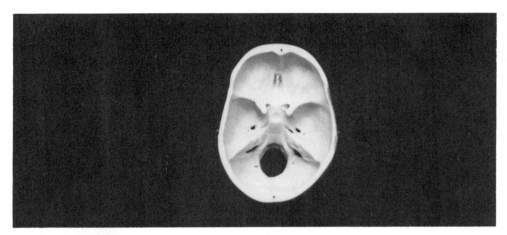

Figure 5.2. Cranium configuration.

There is a stair-stepping design to provide a weight supporting surface for the brain. This also allows the brain to be protected against rolling in the head after an impact. The spheroidal shape provides maximum protection against indentations. The foramen magnum is an opening at the base of the skull through which the spinal cord travels. It permits the elongation of the brain into this area after compressive forces have forced the brain to swell.

There are three brain coverings (meninges) that are important when discussing injuries to the head. The first of these, and the most important, is the dura mater. It is the thick, tough outer lining of the brain, and serves as a structure for the venous sinuses which return blood from the brain to the heart. The middle brain covering, the arachnoid, lies under the dura mater. It derives its name from the Greek words meaning "resembling a spider's web". The third layer and one that lies closest to the brain surface is the pia mater. It is highly vascularized, and dips into all the fulci and fissures of the brain. Between the pia mater and the arachnoid is a space known as the subarachnoid space. The cerebrospinal fluid is contained here.

Mechanisms of Head Injury

Head injuries may be caused in one of the following ways: (1) direct impact; (2) impulsive loading; and (3) static or quasi-static loading. (Torg, 1982) A direct impact may occur in any sport where two bodies collide, or when an object impacts upon the body. The site of the injury generally is recognizable because of the discoloration, swelling, bleeding, or indentation. An impulsive loading, sometimes referred to as accelerative, happens when the body impacts causing a "brain shaking". Falling off a horse and landing on the gluteus maximus may result in whiplash action of the head. The brain collides with the sides of the cranium causing an impairment. No direct contact with the head has been made. A static or quasi-static loading, sometimes referred to as compressive, is a situation in which a constant load is applied to the head. Being crushed under heavy equipment such as a car is an example of this type of head injury. This is not as common in sports as the other two types.

Common Head Injuries

As a result of the impact situations, several injuries may occur to the cranium and the brain. The skull may be abrased, contused, lacerated, or fractured. The brain may be contused or concussed. By far the most severe of these is the concussion.

Table 5.1 defines some of the more common head injuries.

Table 5.1. Common Head Injuries.

Scalp Hematoma	A collection of blood within the layers
Skull Fracture	May be an indentation, simple break, or compound involving a break through the scalp and cranium
Concussion	A clinical syndrome characterized by immediate and transient impairment of neural function. Classified according to length of time of unconsciousness, signs and symptoms

Contusion	Bruising of the brain following a blow
Epidural Hematoma	Bleeding between the cranium and brain coverings, causing a pooling of blood and pressure on the brain; may involve damage to middle meningeal artery
Subdural Hematoma	Bleeding beneath the brain coverings; may be acute or chronic

Mandible and Maxilla

Structure and Function

The mandible, or lower jaw, is the only movable bone of the face. It is joined to the head at the temporomandibular joint (TMJ). An articular disc separates the mandible and the temporal bone. The muscles surrounding this area are used for mastication. Next to the nasal bone, it is the most commonly fractured bone of the face. (See Figure 5.3 a, b, c)

The maxilla is located between the mouth and eyes. It forms the upper jaw, and is sometimes referred to as the cheekbone. It articulates with the frontal, maxillary, and temporal bones superficially, and forms the lateral and inferior rim of the orbit.

Mechanisms of Injury

Injuries to the face generally are the result of direct blows. Collisions with other moving bodies, or stationary objects may lead to contusions or fractures. Anatomically speaking, there is little soft tissue protection for the face. This, in addition to the uneven and jutting surfaces, makes this region vulnerable to injury.

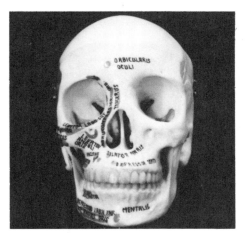

Figure 5.3a
Frontal view of mandible and
maxilla model.

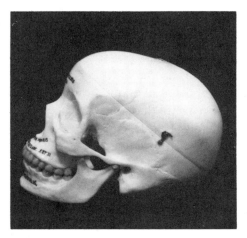

Figure 5.3b
Side view of mandible and maxilla
model.

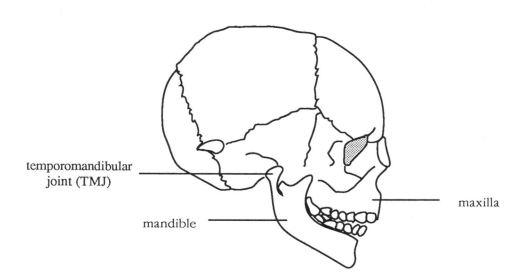

temporomandibular
joint (TMJ)

mandible

maxilla

Figure 5.3c
Side view of mandible and maxilla.

Mandible-Maxilla Injuries

The major injury problem of this area is a fracture. Midface fractures are classified according to the location and are referred to as the LeFort Classification. (See Figure 5.4) LeFort I fractures are horizontal detachments that occur at the level of the nasal floor. LeFort II fractures occur in the midface region. The most devasting fracture is classified as LeFort III and results in a craniofacial disassociation

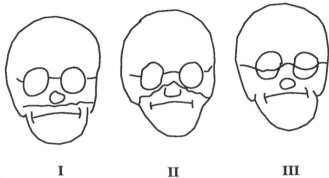

I   II   III

Figure 5.4.
LeFort fracture classification.

Mandibular fractures occur most frequently near the front angle. The next most frequent area is the condylar region.

Nose, Eyes, Ears, Teeth

Mention should be made of the other facial structures which may be affected as a result of direct impacts to the region. Facial injuries can be multiple in nature.

Nose

The nose is composed of two parts: an external portion which is cartilagenous in nature, and an internal portion which is bony in nature. The nasal cavity is separated by the nasal septum, and provides a communication network with the outside environment, with the middle ear, and with the conjunctiva of the eye. This is an important consideration is treating injuries because of the spread of infection. The paranasal sinuses in the skull communicate directly with the nose. Complications from skull fractures may directly affect the sinuses.

Nosebleeds are possible in sport and exercise, some of which may be caused by a direct blow. If the blow is hard enough, a fracture may result. Nose fractures are the most common facial injury.

Eyes

A view of the eye may be seen in Figure 5.5 a, b. The areas most implicated in blunt trauma injuries are the eyelids, cornea, retina, conjuctiva, and orbital floor. The eyelids protect the eye by providing a "curtain" over it, and keeping the cornea moist. The cornea is the anterior transparent part of the eye forming the outer

Figure 5.5a
The eye model.

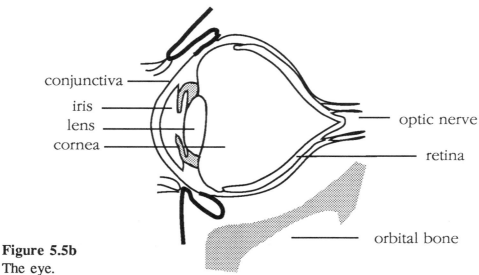

Figure 5.5b
The eye.

coating. The immediate vision instrument of the eye is the retina. It receives the image formed by the lens. The conjunctiva forms the inner lining of the eyelids and covers the white portion of the eye. The orbital bones form the protective encasement for the globe.

There are a number of injuries involving the eye. Some of them are injuries needing immediate referral to a specialist, while others can be treated at the site. Some of the more common eye injuries are described in Table 5.2 along with some possible causes and treatment condition.

Table 5.2. Common Eye Injuries, Causes, and Treatment Condition

Injury	Cause	Treatment
fracture of orbital bone	blow to face	immediate referral
laceration of eyelid	blunt object, broken glasses	immediate referral
foreign body on cornea	high impact object such as a piece of metal	immediate referral
laceration/perforation	errant fish-hook, etc.	immediate referral
hemorrhage in the anterior chamber	blow to face	immediate referral
black eye	blow to face	treated at site
conjuctival foreign body	wind, as in a piece of dirt	treated at site
dislodged contact lens	blow or collision	treated at site
conjunctival hemorrhage	allergy, blow	treated at site

Ears

The ear is composed of three parts. The external portion includes the cartilagenous part which protrudes from the head, the ear canal, and tympanic membrane. The middle ear houses the three otic bones called the malleus (hammer), incus (anvil), and stapes (stirrup). The auditory tube also is located in the middle ear. The inner ear is the location for the cochlea, Organ of Corti, semicircular canals, the acoustic nerve (See Figure 5.6).   Noise-induced hearing loss affects these structures.

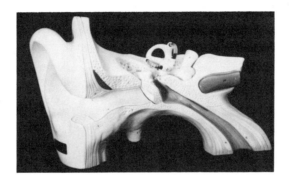

Figure 5.6.
The ear model.

Injuries to the ears are caused by sharp and blunt trauma, environmental pressure and temperature changes, and noise. Typical ear injuries and their causes may be found in Table 5. 3.

Table 5.3. Ear Injuries and Mechanisms of Injury.

sunburn	overexposure to sun rays
frostbite	overexposure to extreme cold
cauliflower ear	repeated trauma (blows) and failure to drain a hematoma
external otitis	infection resulting from exposure to contaminated water
perforated tympanic membrane	blows, foreign objects

otitic barotrauma	perforation of tympanic membrane or hemorrhaging in the ear caused by changes in environmental pressure
tinnitus	ringing in the ear caused by excessive and prolonged exposure to noise

---

Teeth

The teeth may be injured as a result of a direct blow or they may be injured as a result of an indirect blow to another part of the head or face. An example may be getting hit from beneath the chin causing compressive forces on the teeth. The anatomy of a tooth is shown in Figure 5.7.

Figure 5.7.
The tooth.

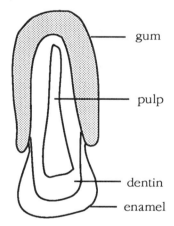

The crown of the tooth extends above the gum, while the root extends below. The hardest substance in the body, enamel, constitutes the outer layer of the crown. Cementum covers the outside of the tooth below the gum. Beneath the cementum and enamel is another hard substance called dentin. The pulp is located at the central portion of the dentin.

Injuries to the tooth may be serious if the pulp of the tooth is damaged. The vascular and nerve supply are found here, and if damaged may result in the loss of the tooth. Partially or completely dislocated teeth may be saved if kept moist and relocated quickly.

The Spine

The spine, or vertebral column, is a unique structure in that it serves several important purposes.

1. It is a series of structures (vertebrae) which give support and stability to the body. This particularly is true in the cervical region where the vertebrae must hold up the head.

2. It permits movement in many directions: flexion, extension, rotation, and lateral bending.

3. It provides a protective casing for the spinal cord.

4. It provides a site for the attachment of muscles.

5. It transfers and attenuates loads to and from the extremities. This is implicated most in sport and exercise injuries.

The spine is composed of 24 vertebrae, the sacrum, and coccyx. The 24 vertebrae further are divided into the cervical region (7), thoracic region (12), and lumbar (5) region. The cervical and lumbar regions are the two areas of most interest to sport and exercise participants.

Structure and Function

The spinal column has four distinct curves. (See Figure 5.8) The thoracic and sacrococcygeal curves are present at birth. The cervical and lumbar curves develop after birth in response to forces placed upon the vertebrae in this region. Interestingly, these latter two curves are involved in most discussions of spinal cord injuries and impairments.

Structurally, the vertebrae have different shapes. The cervical vertebrae are small with the facets oriented at a 45- degree angle. This permits a wide range of motion that includes flexion, extension, lateral flexion, and rotation. The vertebrae in the lumbar region are large with the facets oriented at a 90- degree angle. This permits flexion, extension, and lateral flexion. However, there virtually is no rotation in this area.

Figure 5.8.
Curves of the spine.

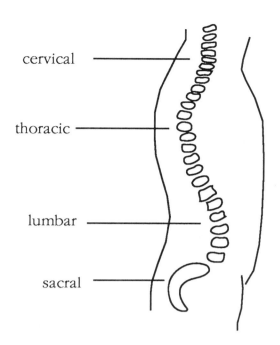

cervical

thoracic

lumbar

sacral

A typical vertebrae (See Figures 5.9a and 5.9b) has some general characteristics. Exceptions to this description are the first (C1) and second (C2) cervical vertebrae. They will be discussed later. The vertebral foramen is a large hole through which the spinal cord passes. Anterior to this is the vertebral body, while posterior to this is the vertebral arch. The arch is formed by two pedicles and laminae. The pedicles arise from the vertebral body, whereas the laminae arise from the pedicles. A spinous process and two transverse processes project posteriorly and laterally. The superior and anterior articular processes unite adjacent vertebrae. Spinal nerves exit from the vertebral column via the intervertebral foramina

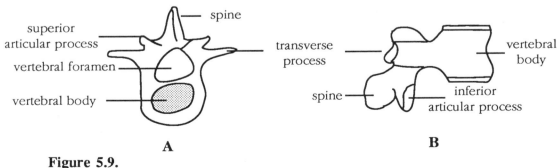

superior articular process

spine

vertebral foramen

vertebral body

transverse process

spine

vertebral body

inferior articular process

A

B

Figure 5.9.
Vertebra as viewed from: (A) above and (B) side.

which are bounded by the vertebral notches of adjacent vertebrae. (Grabiner, 1989) There are two articulations within the vertebral column. One is the articulation between the vertebral bodies and the intravertebral discs. This is classified as a synarthrodial joint because it permits very little movement. The second articulation is between the articular processes of the adjacent vertebrae. This is classifed as a non-axial diarthrodial joint which permits gliding movements only.

Between the vertebral bodies are the intravertebral discs whose primary function is shock absorption. They are composed of a jelly-like substance in the center called the nucleus pulposus, and a stronger fibrocartilagenous outer structure called the annulus fibrosus. There is a criss-cross arrangement of the collagen fibers of the annulus fibrosus that allows it to withstand high bending and torsional loadings. Discs are like water-filled sponges that tend to lose resiliency as the body ages. (See Chapter 7 for further discussion of aging and discs.) The thickness of the discs changes from thin (cervical) to thick (lumbar). This is to accomodate the heavier loads placed on the lumbar vertebrae.

The ligamentous structures provide support and stability for the vertebral column. They must check the displacement of the vertebrae during movement and loading. The major ligaments are the anterior and posterior longitudinal, ligamenta flava, supraspinal (becomes ligamentum nuchae in cervical region), interspinal, and intertransverse. (See Figure 5.10)

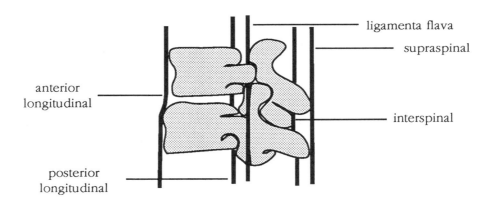

Figure 5.10.
Ligaments of the vertebrae.

There are numerous muscles involved around the vertebral column. They will not be discussed here. However, if a muscle or muscle group is involved in an injury or impairment it will be discussed at that time.

The two atypical vertebrae of the spine are C1 and C2. (See Figure 5.11) C1, also known as the atlas, articulates with the occipital bone of the skull. It is unique in that it has no body. Movements of flexion-extension are allowed. C2, also known as the axis, is identified by its odontoid process (or dens), a phylogenetically displaced body of the atlas. The transverse ligament separates the odontoid process from the spinal cord. Failure of this ligament may mean spinal cord embarassment.

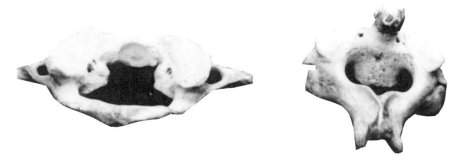

Figure 5.11.
Atypical vertebrae: (A) CI model; (B) C2 model.

Mechanisms of Injury

The mechanisms for injuries to the spinal column are: (1) hyperflexion; (2) hyperextension (sometimes accompanied by rotation); and (3) axial loading. Hyperflexion movements cause some of the more serious injuries in the cervical region. Driving the helmet into the body of an opposing football player is an example of the hyperflexion movement. Hyperextension movements may result from a whiplash, or lifting a heavy weight over the head in weight lifting activities, or rowing in the pull-back motion. The golf swing, especially on the downswing and follow-through, is an example of a hyperextension movement with rotation. Both hyperflexion and hyperextension cause tension and compression forces on the vertebrae.

Axial loading may result from diving into a shallow pool and hitting the head. This is an example of a compressive force. Axial loading also may cause shearing forces on the lumbar vertebrae at the site of the sacrum. LeVeau (1977) discussed the lumbrosacral angle and its relationship to compressive and shearing forces. (See Figure 5.12) He described the vertical forces acting on the lumbar

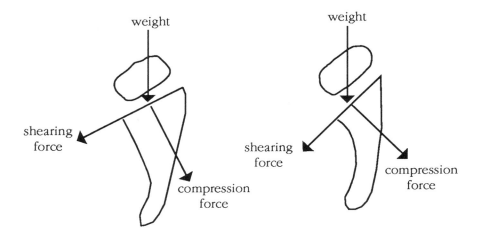

Figure 5.12.
Compression and shearing forces with changes in the lumbrosacral angle.
(Adapted with permission from LeVeau, 1977)

spine as moving in two directions: a compressive force downward, and an anterior shearing force acting across the disc.

There are other causes of spinal column impairments. They include: (1) congenital defects; (2) poor posture; (3) faulty body mechanics; and (3) obesity. (Arnheim, 1985)

Common Spinal Column Injuries and Impairments

The spinal column is subject to the same kinds of soft tissue injuries as any other part of the skeleton. Therefore, those of an unusual nature, or those specific to this region will be described in Table 5.4 The injury and the mechanism of the injury is provided in order to understand the interrelationship between anatomical structure and function of the area.

Table 5.4. Spinal Column Injuries and Mechanisms of Injury.

Injury	Mechanism of Injury
fracture of atlas	indirect trauma from a compression head injury
fracture of odontoid	hyperflexion or hyperextension movement
cervical sprain	hyperextension resulting from a whiplash
cervical burner (nerve stretch)	opposite movement direction of head and shoulder
low back strain	sudden and violent extension contraction, as in incorrect lifting technique
lumbar fracture, compression of anterior body	rapid flexion movements, landing from heights
lumbar fracture, spinous or transverse process	direct blow
lumbar fracture, horizontal vertebral body	rapid and forceful rotation of trunk
disc injuries	anterior shearing forces, aging
spondylolysis (defect or fracture of pars interarticularis)	repeated trauma, stress, heredity
spondylolisthesis (slipping forward of vertebral body over vertebra below)	repeated trauma, stress, heredity

Thorax

The thorax is composed of the sternum and twelve pairs of ribs. It is the most rigid part of the trunk, and gives the upper body stability. Its major function is a protector for the underlying lung and heart structures. It also assists the lungs in inspiration and expiration.

Each of the 12 pairs of ribs articulates with one of the 12 thoracic vertebrae on the posterior side of the body. The first 7 ribs on the anterior side attach to the sternum via the costal cartilage. The 8th, 9th, and 10th ribs unite together through a common cartilage to the sternum. The 11th and 12 ribs are called "floating ribs" because they do not attach to the sternum.

The main mechanisim of injury in the thorax region is a direct blow. Sudden twists or turns, for example a serving motion in tennis, may also cause injuries. Table 5.5 describes several common thorax injuries and mechanisms of injury.

Table 5.5. Common Thorax Injuries and Mechanisms of Injury.

Injury	Mechanism of Injury
rib fracture	direct blow, lack of protective equipment
sternum fracture	direct blow, lack of protective equipment
breast contusion	direct blow, inadequate support
costochondral separation or dislocation	direct blow, fall, twisting
muscle strain	violent stretching due to twisting

The Shoulder

The discussion which follows on the shoulder will include both the shoulder girdle and shoulder joint. The shoulder girdle is composed of the scapula and clavicle, while the shoulder joint is composed of the scapula, clavicle, and humerus.

Structure and Function

Three joints are involved in the shoulder complex. The sternoclavicular joint between the sternum and clavicle, the acromioclavicular uniting with the acromion process of the scapula and the clavicle, and the glenohumeral connecting the humerus and scapula. The bony stability of the sternoclavicular joint is weak. However, it plays an important role in absorbing shock due to trauma. Likewise, the bony stability of the acromioclavicular joint is weak, but it, too, serves as a shock absorber. The glenohumeral is the most freely movable of all of the joints, and is classified as a diarthrodial joint. It is characterized by the ball and socket arrangement which allows movement in several planes: flexion and extension, abduction and adduction, horizontal flexion and extension, and circumduction. (See Figure 5.13a)   The important landmarks are identified in Figure 5.13b.

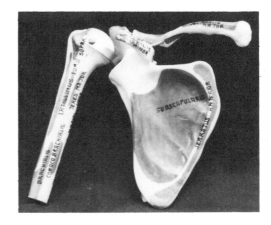

Figure 5.13a.
The shoulder joint model.

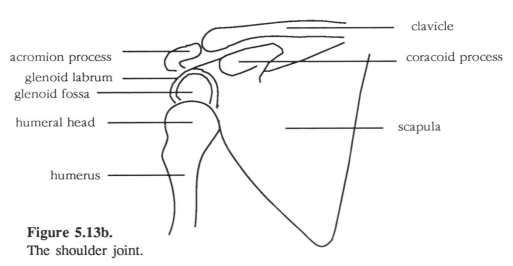

Figure 5.13b.
The shoulder joint.

The stability for the shoulder joint is provided by the ligaments and muscles. The ligaments implicated in shoulder injuries are the acromioclavicular (A-C), the sternoclavicular (S-C), the coracoclavicular (C-C), and the coracoacromial (C-A). The bony architecture provides very little stability because of the great mobility allowed at this joint. The glenoid labrum, a cartilagenous lip, outlines the glenoid fossa to provide the only extra stabilizing structure.

There are a number of muscles which surround the shoulder. The deltoid, pectoralis major, biceps, and rotator cuff (supraspinatus, infraspinatus, teres minor, subscapularis) are mentioned most often in connection with shoulder strains. The other main muscles in this area are the trapezius, latissimus dorsi, serratus anterior, and triceps. See Appendix A (pages 187–189) for location of these muscles and all subsequent mention of muscles in this chapter.

The nerves and arteries in this area, the brachial plexus and brachial artery, are important because they can be damaged when injuries such as dislocations occur. This may have further implications for the lower arm since these structures supply that area.

Mechanisms of Injury

Injuries to the shoulder girdle and shoulder joint result from direct impacts to the area, falls on the point of the shoulder, or overuse. Throwing at excessively high speeds, such as is done in baseball pitching, causes trauma to this area if the muscles are not conditioned properly, range of motion exercises have not been performed before throwing, or proper technique has not been used.

Common Shoulder Injuries

Some of the more common injuries of the shoulder are described in Table 5.6. The mechanisms of injury are included also.

Table 5.6.   Shoulder Injuries and Mechanism of Injury.

Injury	Mechanism of Injury
sternoclavicular sprain	falling on outstretched hand
clavicular fracture	falling on outstretched hand
acromioclavicular strain/tear	falling on point of shoulder, impact with another person
dislocation/subluxation (usually anterior)	initially from a hit with the arm in external rotation, abduction, and elevation
recurrent dislocations	repeated trauma resulting in dislocation or subluxation
rotator cuff tendonitis	overuse, throwing
rotator cuff tears	overuse, throwing, direct blow to shoulder, fall to side or forward on outstretched arm, lifting heavy weights
bursitis	overuse, throwing
bicipital groove tendonitis/ subluxation	repeated microtrauma, ligament laxity
thoracic outlet syndrome	pressure due to extra cervical rib, over-zealous weight lifting, overextension of arm or shoulder, muscle weakness

The Arm and Elbow

The bones of the arm are the humerus, radius and ulna. They form the three joints of the elbow: radiohumeral, ulnohumeral, and radioulnar. (See Figure 5.14a, b)

Figure 5.14a.
The elbow joint model.

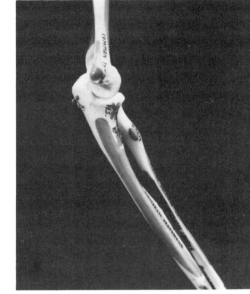

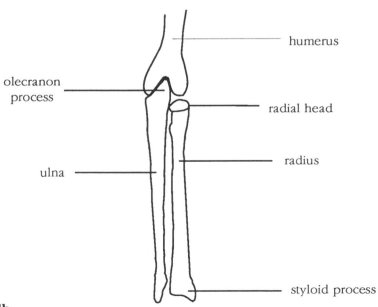

Figure 5.14b.
Posterior view of the elbow joint.

Structure and Function

The elbow joint is characterized by a strong bony arrangement. The olecranon process provides the main source of stability because of its shape and the way it fits around the trochlea of the humerus. The radius, on the other hand, does not function in the same way. Its connection with the humerus is tentative at best, and depends upon the ligaments (ulnar and radial collateral and annular) to provide stability. The joint functions primarily as a hinge joint, but participates in the rotary motions of the forearm.

The muscles surrounding the elbow joint are the flexors (brachialis, brachioradialis, biceps), extensors (triceps), supinator, pronators (teres and quadratus). The major blood supply comes from the brachial artery. Innervation to this area is provided by the median, radial, and ulnar nerves.

Common Arm and Elbow Injuries

Because of the anatomical structure of the elbow joint, most of the injuries involve the bones. In the upper arm where the muscles are located, strains and ruptures are common. Table 5.7 illustrates the common injuries and the mechanisms of the injury.

Table 5.7. Common Injuries of the Arm and Elbow and Mechanisms of Injury.

Injury	Mechanism of Injury
muscle strain/rupture	direct blow, lifting heavy weights
muscle contusion	direct blow
fracture (humerus, radius, ulna)	direct trauma, fall in elbow extension
elbow dislocation	direct trauma, falling on outstretched supinated hand with forearm in extension

epicondylitis	overuse, throwing, improper backhand in tennis
bursitis	direct trauma, chronic irritation
Volkmann's ischemic contracture (claw hand)	compression of vascular and nerve supply around the elbow joint

Wrist and Hand

The wrist joint is formed by the radius, ulna, and carpal bones. The joints of interest are the radiocarpal and the midcarpal. The hand is a complicated structure designed to do many things. The metacarpals and phalanges form the metatarsalphalangeal (MP) joint, the proximal interphalangeal joint (PIP), and the distal interphalangeal joint (DIP). (See Figure 5.15)

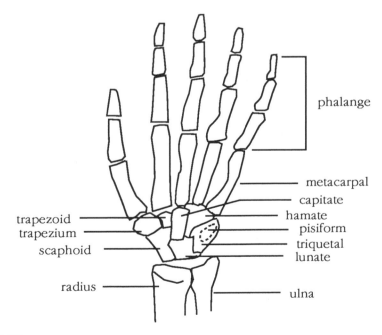

Figure 5.15.
The wrist joint.

Structure and Function

The wrist joint receives its stability from the many ligaments which are found in the area. The muscles controlling the motion of the wrist are located in the forearm, and are known collectively as the flexors and extensors. The movements of the wrist are flexion, extension, ulnar flexion, and radial flexion.

The muscles supplying the hand are divided into two groups: the extrinsic and intrinsic muscles. The extrinsic muscle tendons are located in the hand, but the bellies of the muscles are located in the forearm. The intrinsic muscle tendons arise from the hand.

The ligaments of the hand and fingers are numerous. However, only two are involved frequently in athletic injuries. They are the ulnar collateral ligament of the thumb and the collateral ligaments and the volar plate of the PIP and DIP joints of the fingers.

The fingers move in flexion, extension, abduction, and adduction. The thumb, however, is more versatile. Its movements are flexion, extension, abduction, adduction, circumduction, and opposition (thumb touches tips of fingers).

Mechanisms of Injury

The mechanisms of injury for the hand and wrist are similar to those found in the other structures of the upper limb. They are direct trauma, falling on an outstretched hand, jamming (compressive forces), and overuse.

Common Wrist and Hand Injuries

There are numerous injuries which occur at the wrist and hand. The wrist is susceptible to sprains and fractures because of its ligamentous and bony structure. The fingers, on the other hand, are vulnerable to strains and fractures because of its tendinous and bony arrangements. Table 5.8 describes the common injuries and mechanisms of injury.

Table 5.8. Common Wrist and Hand Injuries and Mechanisms of Injury.

Injury	Mechanism of Injury
Colles' fracture of wrist	falling on dorsally flexed hand, direct blow
navicular fracture	falling on outstretched hand
wrist sprain	hyperflexion or hyperextension of wrist
ganglion	chronic sprain, overuse
"gamekeeper's thumb" (sprain of ulnar collateral ligament)	extreme abduction or hyperextension
PIP sprain	finger pulled to the side
Boutonniere deformity	hyperextension of MP joint, flexion of PIP, hyperextension of DIP due to severe flexion force, direct blow
dislocation of MP joint	jamming due to direct blow
Bennett's fracture	direct blow, falling on hyperextended hand
flexor tendon rupture	flexed fingers forced into extension quickly
mallet finger	compressive force to fingertip, finger forced into hyperflexion
deQuervain's tendonitis	overuse

The Hip and Thigh

The hip joint is an extremely stable joint because it must support the entire body in an upright position. It is formed by the junction between the femur and acetabulum of the pelvis. (See Figure 5.16a, b)

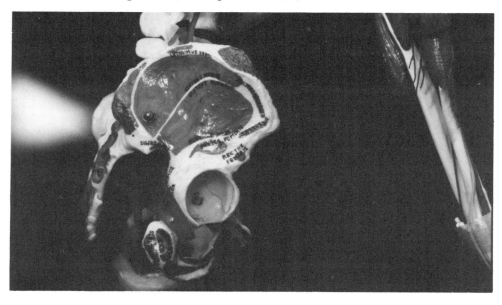

Figure 5.16a.
The hip joint model

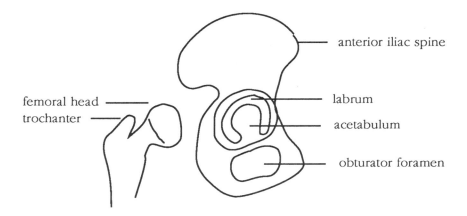

Figure 5.16b.
The hip joint.

Structure and Function

The pelvis is the bowl-like structure of the lower extremity. It is identified by its three parts: ilium, ischium, and pubis. Two important landmarks are the iliac crest, and anterior superior iliac spine. The two ligaments of interest are the iliolumbar and inguinal. The abdominals, erector spinae, gluteals, and rectus femoris provide the musculature around the pelvis.

The hip is considered to be the acetabulum-femur connection. The muscles which contract to produce movement around this joint are the flexors (iliopsoas, pectineus, rectus femoris), extensors (gluteus maximus, hamstrings), abductors (gluteus medius), adductors (adductors, gracilis), lateral rotators, and medial rotators (gluteus medius). The lower extremity is innervated by the sciatic nerve.

Mechanisms of Injury

Because of its strong bony and ligamentous construction, the hip is not particularly vulnerable to fractures and dislocations except for in the elderly. Direct impact to the area, falling, and overstretching are the main causes of injury.

Common Hip and Thigh Injuries

Table 5.9 shows the common injuries of the hip and thigh. Mechanisms of the injury also are described.

Table 5.9. Common Hip and Thigh Injuries and Mechanisms of Injury.

Injury	Mechanism of Injury
iliac crest contusion/ strain (hip pointer)	direct blow, violent tensile strain
hip fracture	direct and violent impact, falling
coccyx contusion	falling directly on coccyx
trochanteric bursitis	overuse, biomechanical deviation, severe exertion
adductor strain	falling with legs in abduction, sudden or severe exertion
quadriceps strain	muscle imbalance, improper warmup, sudden or severe exertion
myositis ossificans (contusion)	direct and severe blow
femoral shaft fracture	direct trauma with heavy forces, possible torsional forces
hamstring strain	muscle imbalance, improper warmup, sudden or violent exertion

The Knee

The knee is the joint most often associated with athletic injuries because of its vulnerablility. A basic description of the joint can assist in understanding why certain injuries occur there. Figures 5.17a, b and 5.18a, b illustrate the structures of the knee.

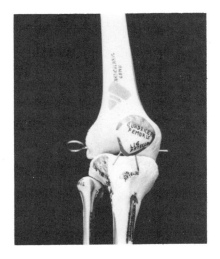

Figure 5.17a.
The anterior view of the knee joint model.

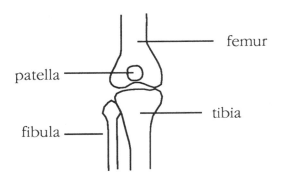

Figure 5.17b.
The anterior view of the knee.

Figure 5.18a.
The posterior view of the knee joint model

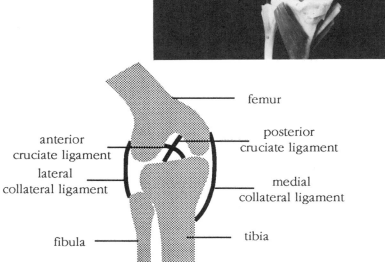

Figure 5.18b.
The posterior view of the knee.

Structure and Function

The knee joint is the articulation between the distal end of the femur and the proximal end of the tibia. The fibula does not articulate with the femur, but does articulate with the tibia forming the tibio-fibular joint. The primary movement of the knee joint is flexion and extension. However, once the knee passes 90 degrees, rotation occurs. That is why this joint is referred to as a condyloid joint rather than a hinge joint.

The ligamentous structure about the knee provides the greatest stabilizing force. The bony arrangement is weak. Strength is needed in this area because of the weight-bearing forces the knee must withstand. The ligaments that help provide this strength are the anterior and posterior cruciates, the lateral and medial collaterals, the popliteal, and the patellar. Each of the ligaments prevents excessive movement in one of the four directions: anterior, posterior, medial, and lateral.

The muscles crossing the knee joint also act at the hip joint. The hamstrings, located on the posterior side of the thigh, flex the knee and extend the hip. The quadriceps, located on the anterior side of the thigh, extend the knee and flex the hip (rectus femoris). The sartorius and gracilis muscles assist in stabilizing the knee on the medial side, while the tensor fascia latae stabilizes on the lateral side. The stabilization from below the knee comes from the gastrocnemius which also is an ankle plantarflexor.

The femur and tibia are separated by cartilage called the meniscus. The functions of the menisci are to provide stability for the leg by deepening the tibial surfaces, prevent impact forces being transmitted up the leg by acting as a shock absorber, and limiting motion by acting as a buffer when the knee extends. The medial meniscus is more firmly anchored than the lateral meniscus because of its connection with the medial collateral ligament.

Mechanism of Injury

The mechanisms of knee injury are many. Probably the most devasting injuries of the knee, cartilage and ligament damage, occur because of direct blows from the lateral or medial sides of the leg, or rotating motions of the leg with the foot planted. Overuse, such as found in running excessively long mileages, or repetitive jumping activies found in basketball, causes unnecessary wear and tear on the joint surfaces. Additionally, biomechanical deviations in the foot (See Chapter 6) and muscle imbalances in the hamstrings and quadriceps muscles can lead to injury problems.

Common Knee Injuries

Injuries to the knee are many and varied. Table 5.10 contains some of the most common injuries and the mechanism of the injury.

Table 5.10. Common Knee Injuries and Mechanisms of Injury.

Injury	Mechanism of Injury
patello-femoral pain	overuse injury due to repetitive activities
chondromalacia	chronic overuse injury due to repetitive activities involving extensor mechanism, muscle imbalance,
iliotibial band friction syndrome	muscle tightness in IT band, biomechanical deviation in lower extremity
patellar tendonitis	repetitive activities
meniscal tear	direct blow on lateral or medial side, rotating leg with fixed foot
collateral ligament tear/ strain	direct blow on lateral or medial side, rotating leg with fixed foot
anterior ligament tear	lower leg forced anterior to femur, rotary forces
posterior ligament tear	lower leg forced posterior to femur
synovitis	overuse injury, post injury
patellar fracture	impact with ground or floor
popliteal tendonitis	running downhill excessively

The Lower Leg, Ankle and Foot

The lower leg is analogous to the lower arm in that it is composed of two bones that articulate with a group of eight other bones. The tibia and fibula are the two bones of the lower leg which unite with the tarsals of the ankle. (See Figure 5.19a, b) The foot, and more specifically the talus, articulates with the tibia and fibula. (See Figure 5.20) These articulations thus, are called the tibiotalar, fibulotalar, and distal tibiofibular joints.

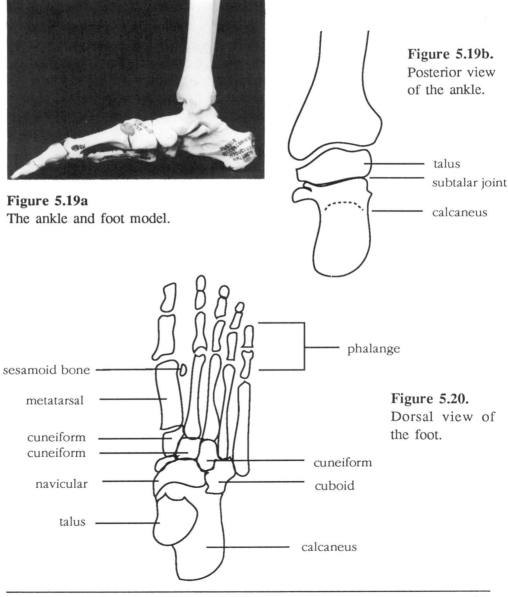

Figure 5.19a
The ankle and foot model.

Figure 5.19b.
Posterior view of the ankle.

talus
subtalar joint
calcaneus

sesamoid bone
metatarsal
cuneiform
cuneiform
navicular
talus

phalange

Figure 5.20.
Dorsal view of the foot.

cuneiform
cuboid

calcaneus

Structure and Function

The ankle joint is a more stable joint that the knee joint because of its mortise configuration. That is, the tibia fits over the talus creating a securely fastenend structure (a mortise). The joint is reinforced by the anterior tibio-fibular, posterior tibio-fibular, external and internal collateral, and interosseus ligaments. For these reasons, the ankle is vulnerable to sprain and fracture injuries.

The muscles influencing the movement of the ankle joint are considered in four compartments. The anterior compartment consists of the tibialis anterior, extensor hallucis longus, and extensor digitorum longus. The deep posterior compartment muscles are the tibialis posterior, flexor hallucis longus, and flexor digitorum longus. The superficial posterior muscles are the gastrocnemius and soleus. They attach to the calcaneus via a common tendon, the Achilles tendon. In the lateral compartment are the peroneals (longus, brevis, tertius). These muscles serve to dorsiflex and plantarflex the foot.

The foot has three anatomic parts: hindfoot (calcaneus and talus); midfoot (navicular, cuboid, cunneiforms); and forefoot (metatarsals and phalanges). The talus is the link between the foot and the lower leg and receives the entire weight of the body. It is characterized by having no muscles attached to it.

The two arches of the foot are the longitudinal (inner and outer) and the transverse. The latter exists only in non-weight bearing situations. The inner portion of the longitudinal arch acts as a shock absorber, while the outer portion is for support.

The most important joint in the foot when discussing foot injuries is the subtalar joint. It is formed by the inferior surface of the talus and the os calcis of the calcaneus. The movements of pronation and supination take place here. Pronation is a combination of dorsiflexion, abduction, and eversion. Supination is a combination of plantarflexion, adduction, and inversion. Four small ligaments reinforce the joint. The other joints are the midtarsal, tarsometatarsal, intermetatarsal, metatarsophalangeal, and interphalangeal.

Mechanisms of Injury

Ankle injuries are of the sprain or fracture type because of the structure of the joint. The mechanisms for sprains or fractures are compressive forces, torsional forces (inversion), and bending beyond the normal limits. Foot injuries tend to be due to vertical loading situations causing compression forces, tensile forces causing sprains, or frictional forces.

Common Lower Leg, Ankle, and Foot Injuries

Injuries of the lower extremity are far more common and numerous than the upper extremity. Compression due to weight bearing activities seem to precipitate more injuries. Table 5.11 describes some of the common injuries with the accompanying mechanisms.

Table 5.11. Common Injuries of the Lower Leg, Ankle, and Foot and Mechanism of Injury.

Injury	Mechanism of Injury
anterior compartment syndrome	repeated microtrauma, biomechanical deviations in lower extremity
shin splints	impact to lower leg, repeated microtrauma, biomechanical deviations in lower extremity
fracture	direct blow, bending or tensile forces
ankle sprain	tensile forces on ligament/capsule due to movement of joint beyond normal limit
Achilles' tendonitis	repeated microtrauma, sudden tensile forces
dislocated peroneal tendon	falling with foot driven under body tendon
plantar fasciitis	sudden turning, biomechanical deviations in lower extremity
retrocalcaneal bursitis	pressure from back of shoe against heel
stress fracture	repeated microtrauma

dorsal exostosis	heredity
bunion	heredity, tight fitting shoes
turf toe	impact with hard surfaces
Morton's neuroma	compressive forces between 3rd and 4th toes
ingrown toenails	improperly cared for nails, tight shoes
sesamoiditis	frictional forces on bottom of foot
calluses	frictional forces caused by pressure on skin
blisters	frictional forces
black toenail	jamming the toe in the shoe

Summary

An attempt has been made in this chapter to interrelate function and structure of the various joints of the body with the mechanism for injury. This knowledge should lead to a better understanding of why injuries of a specific nature occur at one site and not another. Further, this knowledge should lead one to consider measures for the prevention of injuries. For a further discussion of the biomechanics of the skeletal system and specific injuries, their evaluation and treatment, one might peruse such texts as Kreighbaum and Barthels (1985), Arnheim (1985), O'Donoghue (1984), Roy and Irvin (1983), Griffith (1986), and Peterson and Renstrom (1986).

Review Questions

1. How does an understanding of the interrelationship between structure and function of the musculoskeletal sytem and the mechanism of injury benefit someone interested in sport and exercise injuries?

2. Identify the stabilizing factor for each joint discussed and explain what general category of injuries are likely to occur at that joint.

3. Using the information from the previous question, explain what the typical mechanisms for injury would be for each joint.

References

Arnheim, D. D. (1985). Modern Principles of Athletic Training. St. Louis: Times Mirror/Mosby College Publishing.

Grabiner, M. D. (1989). "The vertebral column." In P. J. Rasch, Kinesiology and Applied Anatomy, (pp. 169-192). Philadelphia: Lea & Febiger.

Griffith, H. W. (1986). Complete Guide to Sports Injuries. Tucson, AZ: H P Books, Inc.

Kreighbaum, E. & Barthels, K. M. (1985). Biomechanics: A Qualitative Approach for Studying Human Movement. Minneapolis: Burgess Publishing Company.

LeVeau, B. (1977). Williams and Lissner: Biomechanics of Human Motion. Philadelphia: W. B. Saunders Company.

O'Donoghue, D. H. (1984). Treatment of Injuries to Athletes. Philadelphia: W. B. Saunders.

Peterson, L. & Renstrom, P. (1986). Sports Injuries: Their Prevention and Treatment. Chicago: Year Book Medical Publishers, Inc.

Roy, S. & Irvin, R. (1983). Sports Medicine: Prevention, Evaluation, Management, and Rehabilitation. Englewood Cliffs: Prentice-Hall, Inc.

Torg, J. S., Editor. (1982). Athletic Injuries to the Head, Neck and Face. Philadelphia: Lea & Febiger.

Biomechanics of Anatomical Variations

To some degree we all have skeletal variations which give us advantages and disadvantages for sport and performance. These variations also extend into the predisposition for injury or protection from injury. As the variances become more dramatic, specific patterns of injury can be predicted based on the abnormal biomechanical forces. This chapter describes some of the more common anatomical variations, and the biomechanical considerations they represent.

Scoliosis

Scoliosis is defined as a lateral curvature of the spine. It may be slight and straighten out during forward bending or it may be severe enough that the rotary component remains and is classified as structural. The rotary component is present to some degree in all scoliosis conditions, but it is very evident in the moderate and severe structural deformity. The forward bending test is used as an attempt to straighten out the spine's lateral deviation. When the scoliosis is of a severity that it does not straighten out (structural), there is a rib hump on the convex side of the curve. There may also be limitations in range of spinal motion for side bending to the side of the curve and rotation to the side of the curve. Those deviations and limitations of motion are usually due to the abnormal vertebral joint alignment, but may also be due to the creep phenomenon associated with soft tissue adaptive shortening and lengthening. There is usually a shortening of the muscles and ligaments adjacent to the spine on the concave side of the curve, and also a stretched and weak soft tissue problem on the convex side. This is a good example of how an appropriate stretching and strengthening program can help prevent the loss of function.

The cause of scoliosis may be a congenital wedge deformity of one or more vertebrae, unequal leg length, or injury. Anything but the very mildest curves (with no rib hump) should be referred to a physician for evaluation. X-rays are usually taken and, especially in children, it is important to get base line records for later follow-up to determine if the scoliosis is progressing and may need more than preventative exercise for treatment. (See Figure 6.1.)

It is also important to note that there is usually a compensatory curve either above or below (or both) the main curve. These compensatory curves are Nature's way of biomechanically balancing the forces of the spine, and are actually fairly successful at leveling the shoulders and pelvis. These smaller compensatory curves are not to be ignored however, and are a potential source of pain or mobility limitation unless they are also attended to with appropriate treatment and or exercises (Salter, 1970).

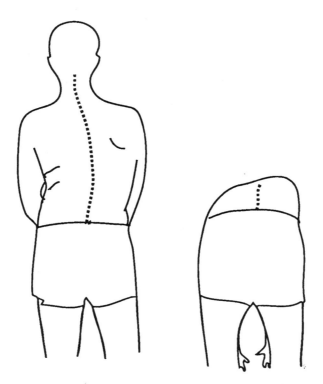

Figure 6.1.
Scoliosis

Scoliosis is a common cause of low back pain as it may cause a pelvic obliquity. This obliquity would then indicate a necessity to evaluate the leg length to determine if a lift is necessary to reduce the stress on the low back. The leg length discrepancy may also be functional or structural. This problem will be discussed in greater detail in the next section.

Biomechanical Lower Extremity Deviation

Throughout this discussion of lower extremity deviation it is important to remember that the entire body represents a dynamic chain of forces which act or react to each other. For example, the excessive pronator will have additional rotary forces going up the chain to the knee, hips, and pelvis which require control and attenuation. These forces are many times magnified by activity and may need to be addressed in a comprehensive manner along several links in the chain. The deviations described in this section are not to be considered as isolated problems to one joint or area, but to the entire system both above and below.

Leg Length

A deviation in leg length may either be a true leg length difference or a functional leg length difference as noted above. A true leg length problem will cause the low back to be under additional stress as the low back attempts to stabilize the resulting pelvic obliquity. It can also cause problems at the hip as it is forced to abduct and circumduct more on the long side than the short side during walking and running gait. The foot may also pronate more on the long side and supinate on the short side to help adjust for the difference in length.

A functional leg length problem may be due to a scoliosis condition and pelvic obliquity. This situation may show up first in the back because of the existing condition above it. The functional leg length deviation may also have the same adjustments at the hip and foot as noted above with the true leg length, but would likely be to a lesser degree.

It is important to note that most people have some leg length differences of 1/2 inch or less. But, deviations greater than this may need attention to prevent problems whether the difference is functional or true.

Pronation and Supination

In the past few years there has been a lot of discussion about excessive pronation and supination of the foot. Shoe companies have responded with new designs to help control pronation or support a foot that is excessively supinated. Unfortunately, not everyone knows what kind of shoe design would match their feet, and they sometimes buy shoes which are wrong for them.

First, it is important to realize that during normal walking or running, there is a normal amount of pronation and supination of the foot which goes on all the time. This is how the foot absorbs shock, accommodates to the weight bearing surface, and gains architectural strength for push off. The subtalar joint is the specific area where the pronation and supination take place. Pronation is associated with the foot abducting, externally rotating, and dorsiflexing. Pronation also causes the calcaneus to evert and move to a position of rear foot valgus. Supination is basically the opposite of pronation. Supination is associated with adduction, internal rotation, and plantarflexion. The rear foot or calcaneus inverts and assumes the rear foot varus position. (See Figure 6.2)

During normal walking gait the foot is in supination at heel strike and then rapidly pronates as soon as weight begins to be accepted. Pronation continues

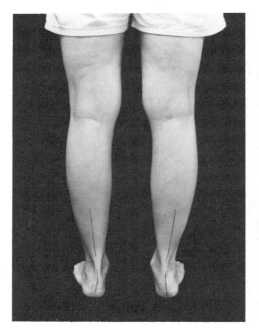
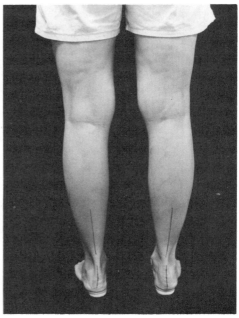

Figure 6.2a.
Rearfoot valgus without orthotics.

Figure 6.2b.
Rearfoot valgus with orthotics.

throughout the weight acceptance until foot flat and toe strike, at approximately 40% of the gait cycle. Supination begins at toe strike and continues through mid stance, toe off, and swing phase.

The function of pronation is to accept the body weight, and at the same time accommodate to the variable weight bearing surface. The foot accomplishes this through the motion of the subtalar joint, as it makes the foot more flexible to attenuate the shock of the weight loading. Then the foot must change from an adaptable shock absorber to a firm and powerful push off device. This happens as supination begins and the joints of the foot tighten up to become a stable base for a solid push off.

With an understanding of the normal pronation and supination functions, it is easier to understand how the excessive pronator or supinator has problems. The excessive pronator either starts too early into pronation or stays too long into mid stance, or both. This causes excessive rotation of the talus, knee, and hip as the rotation continues up the kinematic chain. Excessive pronators may get too much weight bearing at the second metatarsal head, hallux valgus, weak and over stretched soft tissue at the medial ankle, tight lateral ankle soft tissue, patellar compression problems at the knee (from poor tracking), and hip bursitis from excessive rotation. Conversely, the excessive supinator is prone to plantar fasciitis, lateral ankle sprains, shin splints, and ilio-tibial band syndrome. Another generalization is that the excessive pronator usually has a flat foot and gets too much rotation up the chain. Whereas, the excessive supinator usually has a higher arch and does not absorb shock as well and therefore transmits more shock up the chain.

Knee Deviations

The biomechanical variations of the knee to be discussed here include both the patello-femoral and the tibio-femoral joints. Upon considering the tibio-femoral joint, the medial or lateral deviations are referred to as genu (knee) valgus or varus. Colloquial terms are "knock kneed" or "bow legged" respectively. As with most skeletal deviations, the cause is largely inherited from parents with some genetic inclination for these differences. Disease or injury may also be the cause of these alignment deviations.

Genu Valgus conditions are sometimes present due to a slightly longer medial condyle. This pushes the medial tibia down and consequently the lower leg displaces laterally. Injuries such as cartilage damage or disease such as arthritis may also contribute to this type of alignment. The medial knee soft structures become stretched out and the lateral knee soft structures become tight. Also the strength of the knee is compensated due to a poor angle of pull of the quadriceps. Women have this problem more than men, and tall people have it more than those people short in stature.

Genu Varus is the opposite of Genu Valgus, and has a bowed leg appearance as additional stress is present at the lateral knee. The lateral knee structures are stretched out and the medial knee is tight. People with this problem are prone to ilio-tibial band friction syndromes. They also lack some of the rotation that is present in the normal or valgus deformity. Patellar tracking is not as much of a problem in the varus vs. the valgus alignment. Men tend to have genu varus more than women, and short people more than tall. (See Figure 6.3.)

Both the genu valgus and varus conditions may be helped by orthotics in the shoes which help control the medial or lateral pressure at the knee. A generalization which can be drawn is that genu valgus alignments often go along with excessive pronation and the inverse is generally true for excessive supinators.

Deviation at the knee also significantly affects running efficiency. Genu Valgus conditions can cause the lower legs to "fly out" during swing phase. This

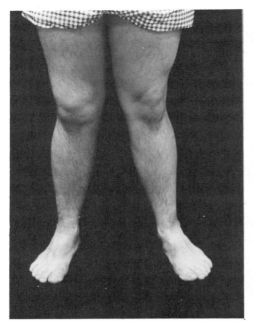

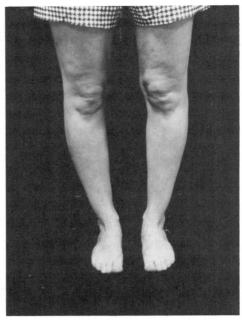

Figure 6.3a.
Genu valgus.

Figure 6.3b.
Genu varus.

takes extra rotation energy of the hips and trunk to control. The Genu Varus condition encourages more lateral shifting and some inefficiency of the thigh musculature as the power line is more difficult to direct straight forward. This is part of the reason that you will find more genu varus in football running backs than you will in distance track men. The running back needs lateral mobility as well as straight forward speed and strength. The distance runner is more concerned with efficient straight forward motion.

The patello-femoral joint is the extension mechanism of the knee. The powerful quadriceps muscle of the thigh focuses its force through the quadriceps tendon, the patella, and the patellar tendon. The patella serves as an assist to elevate the patellar tendon and improve its mechanical advantage as it pulls on the tibial tuberosity. Problems of the patello-femoral joint may be caused by weak lower quadriceps muscles or a structural deviation such as genu valgus or varus. These deviations may cause irritation and pain of the sliding surface of the patella (patello-femoral syndrome), or severe disruption and roughening of the sliding surface (chondromalacia). Other problems common to poor alignment of the patella as it slides in the femoral groove are patellar tendonitis, and subluxing or dislocating patella.

The measurement that is commonly used to determine the alignment of the patella-femoral joint is the quadriceps (or Q) angle. This measurement is derived from intersecting the lines extended from the femur and patellar tendon. Up to 15° is considered normal, and just as women tend to have more genu valgus knee alignments, they also tend to have higher "Q" angle measurements. (See Figure 6.4.)

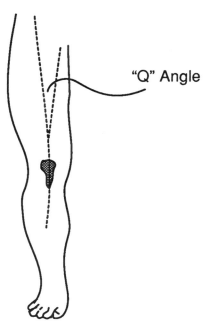

"Q" Angle

Figure 6.4.
The "Q" angle of the knee. The quadraceps or "Q" angle. Formed by intersecting the line extended from the patel-lar tendons and the line of the femur.

Strengthening programs for the lower quadriceps, patellar stabilizing knee supports, and sometimes surgery are necessary to treat these alignment problems, depending on severity.

Hip

There are two alignment considerations for the hip joint. The first is the angle of the neck of the femur to the shaft, and the second is the angle of the femoral head to the femoral condyle.

The first angle (neck-shaft) is a measure of the lateral displacement of the femur away from the pelvis and mid-line of the body. Those with excessive angle are said to have coxa valga, and those with too small an angle are classified as having coxa vara. Adults usually have approximately 125° of neck-shaft angle. The significance of this problem is related also to the kinematic chain below the hip, at the knee and ankle. Coxa valga conditions are prone to having genu varum and excessive supination. Coxa vara conditions are likely to have the inverse, and have genu valga and be an excessive pronator. See the figure below to compare the deviation of the lower extremity with normal. It remains true that the alignment of any deviation at a joint does not require that a compensatory deviation be present above of below, however, postural evaluation will confirm that many do follow the compensatory pattern.

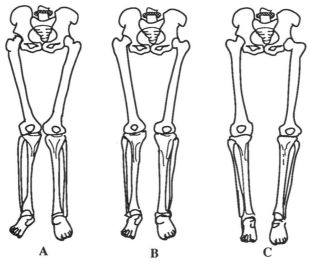

A   B   C

Figure 6.5.
Comparative biomechanical alignments of lower extremities. A) Coxa varus, genu valgus, tarsal pronation B) Normal C) Coxa valgus, genu varus, tarsal supination

The other hip alignment concern involves the angle of the femoral head to the femoral condyle. This assessment indicates the tendency for the hip to be in an internal, external, or neutral position in regard to its rotation. The term which refers to an angle greater than 12 degrees is anteversion. Anteversion also means that the hip is structured to encourage excessive internal rotation during gait, and the inverse is true of retroversion. An example of how anteversion could be a problem is in the activity of dance. Dancers are often required to do turn outs and plié positions in which the hips are at maximum external rotation. A person who already has anteversion of the hips will find it difficult to perform these external rotation maneuvers.

Arthritis

The word "arthritis" literally means inflammation of a joint. There are many types of arthritis but for the presentation of this material we will concentrate on the two most common types. Rheumatoid and osteoarthritis are the major types of arthritis, and although they are similar in some ways, they are very different in others. In pointing out these similarities and differences of rheumatoid and osteoarthritis there will be an emphasis on the biomechanical implications of each type.

Rheumatoid

Rheumatoid arthritis is not a disease that is very often seen in sports medicine clinics. This generalized systemic disease of the connective tissue effects approximately 1% of the population and women three times more often than men. Since rheumatoid arthritis may onset at any age, there are many school age children who are affected. The limitations this disease causes often eliminate the sufferer of this disease from participation in sports. However, there is an increase in awareness of fitness activities that are tolerated, and are actually very therapeutic if managed correctly.

First of all, it is imperative that these individuals be medically managed by a physician. Therapists, trainers and exercise physiologists may assist with input from their specific area of practice, but a team approach, including a physician, is most beneficial.

The exact cause of rheumatoid arthritis is still unknown, but there is an abnormal immune system reaction which inflames and destroys joint connective tissue. In rheumatoid arthritis, the peripheral joints of the upper extremities are usually affected first, but elbows, shoulders, feet, ankles, knees, hips, and spine may also be affected.

The biomechanical considerations are that the joints of persons with rheumatoid arthritis are irritable and easily inflamed by excessive activity. Also, the lack of adequate range of motion work may lead to decreased joint motion. It seems that in the case of rheumatoid arthritis, there is a very fine line between doing too much and too little. That fine line may frequently change due to the disease itself and not as a result of activity. Activities which reduce the weight on joints, yet encourage easy and full range of motion are best. Swimming is usually a well tolerated activity. Care should be taken to avoid repetitious activity which applies pressure to the joint.

The primary biomechanical consideration, besides the prevention of irritating the joints, is that often a loss of full range of motion is present, even in the best managed cases. Altered joint function will decrease balance, power, and coordination. The major joint deformations usually involve genu valgus, hallux valgus, and flexion contractures of the hips, knees, elbows, and wrists. The hand and fingers are sometimes the most profoundly affected and should be protected against the ulnar direction pressures that contribute to greater deformity. Hand function such as throwing, gripping, and striking may be significantly reduced.

Osteoarthritis

Osteoarthritis is a degeneration process that affects many more people than rheumatoid arthritis, at an older age. osteoarthritis is a more predictable disease because it effects major weight bearing joints, and is directly related to the amount of wear and tear that the involved joint had to withstand over the years of use. The articular cartilage becomes softer and does not respond to mechanical pressure with the same resiliency as it did at a younger age. Cracks and fissures in the cartilage are formed and the area of focused stress becomes thinner and may completely wear away until subchondral bone surfaces come in direct contact with each other. The peripheral cartilage may thicken and ossify to become a bony lip or osteoplyte at the edge of the joint.

Besides the slowly increasing pain and discomfort with use of the joint, there may also be considerable joint "noise" as it pops, cracks, and grinds. This joint crepitus may be present before pain is evident, and it is often not a reliable measure of the severity of the arthritis. Pain, however, should not be ignored, and rest and management by a physician who can take appropriate x-rays and prescribe medication is required.

The challenge to those involved in advising appropriate exercise is to maintain range of motion and strength in the joint, but avoid repetitive weight bearing activities. Just as with rheumatoid arthritis, swimming is usually well tolerated. Also cycling is an activity which the osteo arthritic person can often handle well. Even though cycling requires repetitive motion, it is with significantly reduced weight bearing.

The hips and knees, along with the lumbar spine, are the major joint areas where this degenerative type of arthritis causes limitation of motion and pain first. These types of joint changes make it more difficult to participate in sports that require a lot of bending and stooping such as handball. However, activities such as running may not be tolerated well either because, besides the fact that it is a high shock and weight bearing activity, there is a relatively small amount of the total joint surface used. The surgical approach for the pain of severe osteoarthritis is often a total joint replacement of the hip or knee. These patients generally do very well post operatively, but the range of motion after rehabilitation remains somewhat limited even though the major problem of joint pain is solved. Therefore, the return to full active sports still is not usually approved. However, modified activity may be well tolerated, and even recommended.

Aging and Potential Injury Problems

From birth to approximately 18 years of age, the body triples in length. An accelerated growth spurt occurs between the ages of 11 and 15. Girls experience the growth spurt much earlier than boys (11-13 years of age and 13-15 years of age, respectively). The growth rate decelerates after about the age of 15, but adult maturation is not reached until about the age of 20 for females and about the age of 25 for males. This is about the time the last epiphyseal growth center has ossified. From then on anatomical and functional changes in the opposite direction occur.

The injury problems in the older, or aging, adult are not all that different from the younger population. However, the potential for those injuries increases because of the functional limitations of the musculoskeletal system. It should be noted that lack of activity coupled with changes in the musculoskeletal structure and function create a greater risk for injury than active participation in exercise and changes in the musculoskeletal structure and function. A general consensus of opinion by several authorities supports the notion that aging cannot be stopped, only slowed down by exercise.

An examination of the musculoskeletal changes that occur with aging would serve to understand the potential areas for concern. Those structures which show changes in aging are bone, cartilage, ligaments, tendons, muscles, and intervertebral discs. Other changes which may increase the risk for injuries are weight and height changes, neuromuscular changes, and vision changes.

Alterations in Bone and Cartilage Structure

Bone changes begin at about the age of 40 years. Remember from the earlier discussion on bone composition (Chapter 3), bone is composed of 30%

organic material and 70% mineral. Collagen makes up 95% of the organic portion. The porosity of the bone is determined by the amount of cortical and trabecular bone present. Cortical bone is stiff and can stand greater stresses, but less strain before failure. Trabecular bone is less stiff than cortical bone, can withstand less stress, but has more strain.

At about the age of 40 years, changes begin to appear in the bone tissue structure. Females will lose about 35-40% of the cortical bone and 55-60% of trabecular bone over a lifetime. Males lose two-thirds of these amounts. A slow phase of cortical bone loss (.3% - .5%/year) begins in both sexes at about age 40. Following menopause, women lose cortical bone at the rate of 2-3%/year. It then reverts to baseline levels after 8-10 years. The slow phase of trabecular bone loss begins about 5-10 years earlier than cortical bone, and occurs in greater magnitude. A range of 4% - 8%/year occurs for 5-8 years following menopause. The skeletal mass may be reduced to 50% of what it was at age 30. This figure is somewhat higher than other reports of 30% in osteoporitic situations. The implication of these alterations in bone tissue composition is in its strength capabilities. Bone strength is proportional to the square of the apparent density. Thus, the potential for fracture type injuries increases. (Kaplan, 1987)

Yamada, as cited by Rogers (1982), has provided some additional data regarding the strength of bones. The greatest tensile, compressive, torsional and bending strength in bones occurs between the ages of 20-29, after which it tapers off. Males and females were found to follow similar patterns, except in bending strength where females were less than males. Yamada further looked at the aging rates for human locomotor tissues. He concluded that cartilage has the fastest aging rate, followed by skeletal muscle, bone, and lastly tendon.

Several precautions should be taken when using the figures presented on bone loss. Remember that bone loss among individuals is variable. Factors which determine the rate of bone loss are: (1) diet; (2) disease; (3) physical activity; and (4) estrogen and testosterone production.

The major consequence of bone loss is a condition known as osteoporosis. Kaplan (1987) defines it as "a generic term referring to a state of decreased mass per unit volume (density) of normally mineralized bone." He further adds, "Osteoporosis is the most common skeletal disorder in the world and is second only to arthritis as a leading cause of musculoskeletal morbidity in the elderly". When bone formation (Wolff's Law, Chapter 3) lags behind bone resorption, there is a weakening in the skeletal framework. This predisposes the individual, primarily a woman, to compressive fractures of the vertebrae, and fractures of the ribs, proximal femur and humerus, and distal radius. Prevention of this condition occurring or progressing can be accomplished by controlling the risk factors associated with it. They are reducing stress in one's life, abstaining from smoking or drinking alcoholic beverages, exercising, including calcium and protein products in the diet, and avoiding excessive consumption of soft drinks. (Marion Laboratories, 1984)

Cartilage, as described in Chapter 3, has two major functions: (1) to absorb the shock of compressive forces between bones; and (2) to minimize the friction and wear between bone surfaces. As described earlier in Chapter 3, cartilage is composed of 80% water, and is considered to have low permeability capabilities. Permeability is a measure of the resistive force required to cause the fluid to flow at a given speed through a porous permeable material (Mow, et al., 1989). The lower the permeability, the more resistance occurs. Thus, the cartilage maintains its shock-absorbing abilities. With aging, the permeability increases.

With reduced permeability and the associated loss of cartilage stiffness, the joints can no longer withstand the stresses they once were capable of. The degree of wear and tear caused by the stresses depends upon the amount of the load and how it is distributed. Mechanical deterioration results because of the imbalance between the stresses applied to the joint and the ability of the tissues to resist the stresses.

Mow et.al. (1989) proposed several hypotheses for describing cartilage degeneration. They said that failure progression relates to: (1) the magnitude of the imposed stresses; (2) the total number of sustained stress peaks; (3) changes in the intrinsic molecular and microscopic structure of the collagen-PG (proteoglycan) matrix, and (4) changes in the intrinsic mechanical property of the tissue. Additionally, the most important failure-initiating factor appears to be a loosening of the collagen network. This leads to the reduced cartilage stiffness, increased permeability, and increased wear and tear.

The result of the mechanical deterioration of the joint is a condition known as osteoarthritis. It has been estimated that 40,000,000 adults have radiographic evidence of osteoarthritis in their hands and feet. Further, it was estimated that 85% of the people between the ages of 70 and 79 showed evidence of osteoarthritis, especially in the spinal column. (Radin & Martin, 1984.)

A research review by Panush and Brown (1987) summarized the factors which may be associated with the development of sports- related osteoarthritis (OA). See Table 6.1.

Controversy still exists regarding participation in sports, competitive or recreational, and the development or aggravation of osteoarthritis. Longitudinal studies on the long-term effects of sport/exercise participation are not in abundance. At this juncture, it would seem logical to assume that the benefits of exercise outweigh the possible damages to the musculoskeletal system which may occur. With better methods of identifying pre- disposing factors to joint deterioration, better training methods, and better rehabilitation methods, the likelihood of any permanent damaging condition in the joints can be reduced.

Table 6.1. Factors which may be associated with development of sports-related osteoarthritis (OA)

Physical characteristics

Age	Early participation may increase risk of OA
Gender	OA may be reduced in osteoporotic post menopausal females with exercise
Ethnic background	Increase OA in Eskimos, decreased OA of hips in the Chinese population
Body habitus	Obesity may increase OA of the knee
Congenital abnormalities (i.e. dislocations)	May increase risk of premature OA at the hip

Biomechanical factors

Gait	May alter normal cartilage stress sites of weight-bearing joints
Joint alignment	Genu varum deformity may increase OA at the knee
Ligamentous instability (i.e. injury)	Increased risk of OA
Impact stress loading degeneration	Increased risk of OA due to chondrocyte degeneration
Immobilization	Increases articular degeneration (fibrillation) which may increase OA
Overuse syndrome	May increase articular degeneration earlier in life

| Prior injury | May increase risk of OA |

Biochemical factors

Aging of articular cartilage	Loss of biophysical properties of articular cartilage (i.e. chondrocytes) may increase risk of OA
Subchondral microfracture	May evolve with repetitive strenuous exercise and later increase risk of OA
Bone growth / remodeling	May be decreased at site of previous fractures; remodelling may be affected by chronic exercise
Joint lubrication	May be decreased with excessive impact loading stress and later increase risk of OA
Local inflammation	May increase risk for development of early OA post-injury
Hormonal influences (i.e. steroids)	An imbalance may affect bone metabolism in such a way as to increase the risk of OA
Synovial fluid characteristics	Alterations in hyaluronic acid, sulfates, structural glycosaminoglycans and water content may increase risk of OA

Characteristics of playing surface

Asphalt	May increase OA
Clay	Unknown
Cement (concrete)	Increases stress-loading, which may increask risk of OA
Grass	May decrease injury and thereby decrease risk of early OA
Ice	Unknown

Tartan surface (Astroturf)	May increase risk of injuries (i.e. turf toe) which may increase risk of premature OA
Water	May decrease the risk of OA by lessening stress and loading
Wood	May increase lower extremity injuries, which may increase risk of OA

Characteristics of Sport

Contact vs. non-contact	May increase of OA with repetitive stress loading
Duration of participation	May increase injuries and development of premature OA

Onset and level of participation

Childhood / adolescent	May increase long term risk of OA
Adult	May increase risk of OA with overuse syndrome
Professional / competitive / amateur / recreational	An increased risk of OA may be associated with antecedent recreational injuries or length of participation

Miscellaneous

Nutritional

protein diets	May cause electrolyte loss and accelerate osteoporosis
phosphate loading	Unknown effect, may deplete magnesium sources
Calcium deficient diets	May increase osteoporosis which may increase risk of OA

Medical therapy	Accurate diagnosis and management of injury may decrease OA
Pharmacological therapy	Certain non-steroidal anti-inflammatory drugs and steroids may have deleterious effects on cartilage. Ice, heat, and rest may decrease local inflammation and decreases risk of OA
Surgical therapy	Surgically or biomechanically altered joints may be more susceptible to OA (i.e. menisectomies) yet allow the individual to continue participation

Preventative measures

Coaching methods	Proper techniques may decrease stressload, prevent injury and therefore OA
Conditioning techniques	Well conditioned athletes may have a decreased risk of OA
Training techniques	Overuse may increase risk of OA
Equipment design (i.e. headgear, shoes)	May decrease OA by decreasing stressloading or preventing injuries
Rehabilitation of injury (i.e. orthotics)	May increase risk of OA and reinjury
Restricted participation post-injury	May decrease risk of premature OA in unstable, injured joints
Rule changes	Will hopefully decrease incidence of injuries and risk of OA

Source: Parush, R. S. and Brown, 1987. Reprinted with permission.

Ligaments and Tendons

Ligaments and tendons have elastic properties which allow them to be stretched and then returned to their original shape. As aging progresses, greater deposits of non-elastic fibrous tissue are made, thus causing greater stiffness. The rebounding capabilities of the structures is decreased.

The ligaments in the spinal column region generally are inelastic in nature because of a high collagen content. This serves as a protection for overstretching and excessive tensile forces. The ligamentum flavum, which reinforces the vertebral arches, is an exception. It has extreme elasticity. During extension movements, it contracts; while during flexion movements, it lengthens. This gives the intrinsic portion of the spinal column stability. As an individual ages, this structure also becomes fibrous and begins to lose its resiliency.

Muscles

Aging muscle loses strength and contractile qualities. There is a marked loss in number and size of muscle fibers. This, along with an increase in collagen and fat, contributes to a decline in efficient muscle function.

The antigravity muscles (erector spinae, gluteals, abdominals, quadriceps, and triceps surae) play a role in maintaining an upright posture. As aging progresses a greater amount of postural sway is evident. More work is needed by the antigravity muscles which already are weakened due to the aging process.

Intervertebral Discs

The intervertebral discs located along the spinal column function to withstand compressive forces and to distribute the loads placed upon the vertebrae. The inner portion of the disc, the nucleus pulposus, is constructed of a gelatin-like mass and is very fluid in nature. During the aging process, the discs lose their water-binding capacity and become dehydrated. As the disc becomes drier, it loses the ability to stretch, store and distribute loads. The outer portion of the disc, the annulus fibrosus, is much tougher because it is constructed of collagen fibers. The fibers are arranged in a criss-cross pattern to accommodate high bending and torsional loads. The older the person becomes, the shorter in stature he/she becomes because of the degenerating discs.

It has been shown that young people can withstand compression forces of 635 kg (1398.77 lb). It reduces to 158.8 kg (349.77 lb) in older people (Morris, 1973). This makes the older person more susceptible to spinal column injuries when lifting heavy objects or performing activities which place compressive stresses on the vertebrae.

Prevention of Injuries in the Aged

Aging is the body's decreased ability to adapt to the environment. This is Nature's way of telling the aging individual that he/she is "slowing" down. However, not all individuals react in the same way to aging. Some remain active in sport/exercise and only notice subtle changes taking place. Others quite noticeably have restricted ability to move effectively in their environment.

Prevention of injuries for the aging is one of activity modification to fit the present level of functional efficiency. Keeping active and in good physical condition is the other key to reducing injury risk. Walking can replace jogging, low impact aerobics can replace high impact activities, and individual sport activities (e.g. tennis, golf) might be more desirable than team activities (e.g. basketball, soccer). For the previously active and competitive individual, modifying activity level may be a psychological adjustment. Otherwise, the injury prevention guidelines for any age group should apply to the aging as well.

Youth and Potential Sports Injury Problems

Sports participation, be it organized or recreational, is a major part of a young child's life. Accompanying the child's desire to be active is the potential risk of being injured. Epidemiological studies on injury incidence in young children is somewhat inconsistent. Estimates of injury incidence vary from 3% to 22%. Methodological problems account for most of the inconsistencies. However, there is some evidence to suggest that approximately 10% of all sport injuries in young children involve the growth centers of the skeleton (Pappas, 1983).

Young children, pre-adolescents and adolescents, have special injury problems involving the growth plate because their bones have not matured fully, and muscles have not reached their potential in strength development. The ligaments and fibrous capsule surrounding the joints are two to five times stronger than the metaphyseal-epiphyseal junction, or the growth center of the bone (Larson and McMahan, 1966).

Physiology of Bone Growth

By definition, an epiphysis is a secondary bone forming center separated from a parent bone by cartilage. As growth proceeds, it becomes a part of the larger (parent) bone (Thomas, 1978).

There are two types of epiphyses which exist in the appendages of the body, pressure and traction. (See Figure 6.6)

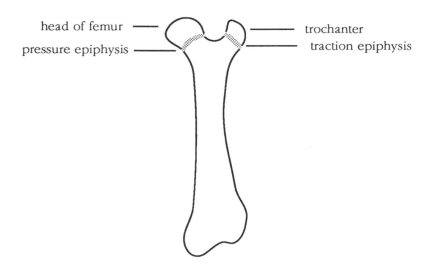

head of femur — pressure epiphysis

trochanter — traction epiphysis

Figure 6.6.
Pressure and traction epiphyses.

Pressure epiphyses are found at the ends of bones which form a joint. They are sometimes referred to as articular epiphyses. It is at the epiphyseal plate region of the pressure epiphyses where the bone lengthens during growth. It is subjected to pressures which are transmitted through the joint. Traction epiphyses are found where muscles attach to the bones. It does not contribute to the bone lengthening process. It is subjected to tensile forces rather than pressure/compressive forces.

The epiphyseal plate, also called the growth plate, is where the separation between bone and cartilage occurs. (See Figure 6.7)

It consists of four zones of cells: (1) zone of resting cells; (2) zone of proliferating cells; (3) zone of hypertrophied cells; and (4) zone of endochondral ossification.

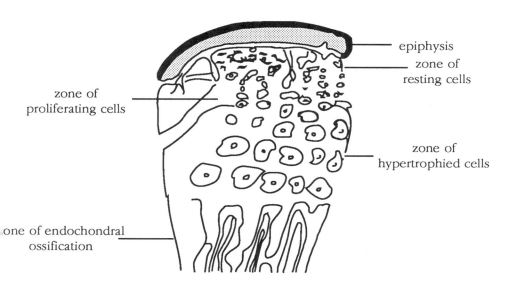

zone of proliferating cells

epiphysis

zone of resting cells

zone of hypertrophied cells

zone of endochondral ossification

Figure 6.7.
Cellular structure of the epiphyseal plate. (Adapted with permission from Larson, 1973)

The zone of resting cells lies immediately adjacent to the epiphysis, and is composed of compact cartilage cells. The zone of proliferating cells is where cell division occurs. Collagen, a fibrous insoluble protein, is found among the cartilagenous material. It serves to give strength and reinforcement to this area. When the cells begin to hypertrophy and arrange themselves in vertical columns, the zone becomes known as the zone of hypertrophied cells. This is where calcification first begins. It also is the weakest portion of the epiphyseal plate. If a separation in the epiphyseal plate is to occur, it does so at this point. After the cells hypertrophy and degenerate, osteoblasts appear to complete the process of bone formation.

Two separate systems of blood vessels are evident in the epiphysis. One system appears in the zone of resting cells, while the other is located in the zone of endochondral ossification. If either of these systems is damaged, disruption in the normal growth pattern is likely to occur. Generally, a separation through the zone of hypertrophied cells, the weakest part of the epiphyseal plate, does not interfere with the blood supply. Thus, normal growth and development of the bone should continue.

Types of Epiphyseal Injuries

Epiphyseal injuries may be of two types: sudden trauma or overuse. Sudden trauma commonly is of the fracture type because of the weak bony structure in relation to the strong ligamentous structure.

Epiphyseal Fractures

A classification system for epiphyseal fracture injuries was developed by Salter-Harris, 1963. (See Figure 6.8)

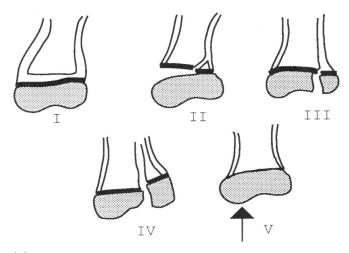

Figure 6.8.
Salter-Harris classification system for epiphyseal fracture injuries. (Adapted from Salter and Harris, 1963.)

Type I injuries involve a complete separation of the the epiphysis from the metaphysis (growing portion of a bone), but no break in the periosteum of the bone. The interface between the metaphysis and epiphysis is contoured to give it strength in resisting separation. However, in the younger child the growth plate is thick which causes the interfacing to weaken. This makes the plate susceptible to shearing and avulsion forces. Therefore, younger children are more susceptible to the Type I injury.

Type II injuries cause a separation along the epiphyseal plate along with a triangular-shaped fragment (Thurston Holland's sign) through the metaphysis.

The periosteum is torn away on one side of the bone, but remains intact on the other side. It is the most common of the epiphyseal plate injuries, and usually is caused by a shear or avulsion force. It usually is seen in children over 10 years of age. The prognosis for Type I and Type II injuries is good because reduction is relatively simple and the blood supply generally is not disrupted.

Type III injury, fortunately not very common, is a fracture which extends from the joint surface to the epiphyseal plate and then along the plate to the periphery of the bone. It often occurs because of a shearing force. Open reduction sometimes is necessary. The reduction must be accurate to avoid incongruency in the joint surface. The prognosis is good if the blood supply is intact and the reduction has been accurate.

Type IV injury is another intra-articular fracture which extends from the joint surface through the epiphysis and epiphyseal plate into the metaphysis. Open reduction almost always is necessary. Accuracy in reduction is essential to prevent premature cessation of growth.

Type V injury is a compression injury in which the epiphysis is crushed against the epiphyseal plate forcing it into the metaphysis. Of all types of epiphyseal injuries, this one has the worst prognosis. The crushing nature of the injury causes a disruption of blood supply. Fortunately this is a rather uncommon injury.

Osteochondroses

Overuse injuries occur as a result of repeated microtrauma to musculoskeletal structures during times of skeletal development. In this regard, it is no different than overuse injuries in adults (e.g. shin splints, stress fractures, chondromalacia, tendinitis, etc.). However, there are several characteristic overuse injuries found in young children because they involve the growth centers. Some of these injuries may be a direct result of repetitive trauma (e.g. Little League Elbow), while others may be the result of some pre-existing condition aggravated by repetitive trauma (e.g. Legg-Calvé-Perthes' disease). Collectively, this group of overuse injuries may be called osteochondroses because they involve degenerative changes in the ossification centers of the epiphyses of bones. If left untreated, the blood supply needed for bone growth is diminished with resulting necrosis (death) of bone. Osteochondroses have been classified into several categories: articular (subchondral) or compression, articular (chondral) or dissecans, nonarticular or traction, and physeal or longitudinal growth (Pappas, 1989). Generally, they are characterized by a painless limp, an alteration of joint function, or pain associated with activity or injury. Following are examples of the more common osteochondroses found in young children.

Legg-Calvé-Perthes'.   One of the most common examples of an articular osteochondrosis is Legg-Calvé-Perthes' disease, also known as coxa plana. It is a hip disorder which occurs in children between the ages of 4 and 10, with a peak incidence at about 6 years of age. It is characterized by a flattened femoral head due to a lack of, or a poor blood supply. Weight bearing activities which cause a compression of the femur on the acetabulum aggravates this condition. The child may have a limp with no pain or pain in the groin area, anterior thigh or knee. There may be stiffness when attempting to internally rotate the hip. Sometimes a spasm occurs in the adductor muscles which makes it difficult to abduct the hip. Muscles on the affected thigh and buttocks also may atrophy. If left untreated, range of motion may be severely retarded, permanent deformity may result, or osteoarthritis may form. It is imperative that this condition be recognized and treated as early as possible. Younger children have greater success rates in the treatment of this disorder. Weight bearing activities should be avoided until the child is pain-free, spasm-free, and has regained normal range of motion.

Slipped Capital Femoral Epiphysis.   This is a less common form of osteochondroses, but one which exhibits similar symptoms as Legg-Calvé-Perthes'. There is pain involvement, usually after a direct trauma, and an accompanying limp. It is most often centered about the knee joint. There is stiffness about the hip joint, and limited motion in hip internal rotation. The cause of the pain, limping, and stiffness is a displacement of the epiphyseal plate at the head of the femur. The exact cause for this condition is not known. However, it has been suggested that a weak bony structure, endocrinological problems, or a pituitary dysfunction may be responsible (Gould and Davies, 1985). Surgery may be prescribed to close the plate.

Osteochondritis Dissecans.   This is another form of osteochondroses which implies a "loose body" or a fragment of cartilage within a joint. One of the most common sites in young children is the posterolateral aspect of the medial femoral condyle, but the ankle, elbow, or hip also may be affected. Whether or not this condition is caused by repeated trauma to an area causing necrosis of the bone, or an existing necrosis is disturbed by a sudden trauma to the area is debatable. Some have suggested the etiology of the condition to be one of bone ischemia, a pre-existing skeletal abnormality associated with endocrine dysfunction, body type, or heredity. When the knee is affected, the child experiences pain and swelling around the joint. There is a noticeable external rotation to the knee during walking. Sometimes there is a feeling of joint locking. The prognosis for successful treatment is better the younger the child is. The more mature the individual becomes, the more likely surgical intervention is needed.

The capitellum of the elbow may be affected from a throwing motion or from certain gymnastic movements. Compressive and shearing forces tend to cause vascular impairment and loose bodies in the joint.

Little Leaguer's Elbow.   Little Leaguer's Elbow is a term given to a non-articular epiphyseal injury. It occurs on the medial epicondyle of the elbow where the flexors and pronators of the arm are attached. By definition, it also is a form of osteochondritis dissecans. The child usually complains of pain on the medial side of the elbow due to the high compressive, shearing, and tensile forces that are generated during the throwing motion. The older the athlete becomes, or the longer it takes to diagnose the condition, the more difficult it becomes to treat. In many cases, surgical intervention means the end of a career in that sport.

Osgood-Schlatter's Disease.   Osgood-Schlatter's Disease, more appropriately a condition rather than a disease, probably is the most common of the non-articular osteochondroses. Tensile forces due to the strong contraction of the quadriceps causes pain at the site of the anterior tibial tubercle. The child usually complains of pain after activity in which the quadriceps have been involved. Repeated tensile forces may cause an enlargement at the site which is painful if palpated. Rest along with strengthening of the quadriceps and stretching of the hamstrings may be the first line of treatment.

Scheuermann's Disease.   This condition also is called Kyphosis Dorsalis Juvenilis. It is a growth plate injury affecting the developmental process of the vertebrae. A kyphosis of the spinal column with lordosis of the lower back is caused by a wedging of the thoracic vertebrae. It becomes worse with exercise involving forward flexion of the trunk. Adolescents, ages 12-15, are affected most frequently. A hyperextension brace and restricted activity may help in alleviating this condition.

Blount's Disease.   Blount's Disease is another growth plate problem involving the medial posterior portion of the proximal tibial epiphysis. If left untreated, it causes an alteration in the growth pattern and varum rotational deformity of the proximal tibia. Surgical intervention is often indicated.

Commonly Injured Epiphyses

The long bones of the extremities are involved in epiphyseal injuries. Injuries occur most often at the distal radius, phalanges, distal and proximal humerus, distal femur, distal tibia, and distal fibula. Examples of the site of the injury and the sport associated with it are given below:

Site	Sport
distal radius	gymnastics
phalanges	gymnastics
distal humerus	baseball pitching
proximal humerus	weight lifting
distal femur	football valgus stress
distal tibia	soccer inversion stress
distal fibula	soccer inversion stress

Prognosis for Epiphyseal Injuries in Young Children

The severity of epiphyseal injuries depends upon the chronological and skeletal age of the child and the duration of the symptoms. The majority of epiphyseal injuries occur at the onset of the adolescent growth spurt. Sometimes they are misdiagnosed as sprains which causes a delay in the treatment of the condition. The encouraging news is that the injuries usually are not severe, and usually do not result in permanent deformities.

Position Statements

Two areas of concern in youth sports participation have received more publicity than any other. They are weight training and long distance running. Several professional groups have been active in formulating policy statements regarding participation in these activities. Among those groups active in formulating the statements are the American Orthopaedic Society for Sports Medicine (AOSSM), American Academy of Pediatrics (APA), American College of Sports Medicine

(ACSM), National Athletic Trainers Association (NATA), National Strength and Conditioning Association (NSCA), President's Council on Physical Fitness and Sports, US Olympic Committee (USOC), and the Society of Pediatric Orthopaedics (SPO). Position statements on running, weight training, and competitive sports may be obtained by writing the individual sports medicine groups.

Prevention of Injuries

In general, injuries in young children can be prevented by using common sense. The bones of young children cannot withstand the same kind of stresses that adults can. Therefore, they should not be expected to compete in adult activities. Running long distances such as the marathon should not be encouraged. Weight training has been found to be beneficial, but should be attempted only with supervision and good training techniques. Power lifting (lifting the maximum weight possible in one repetition) should be avoided. Caution should be used in promoting high impact sports. Remember, too, that children may not be physiologically or psychologically able to participate in high level competition.

Pregnancy and Sex Related Differences

Although men and women are biomechanically more alike than different, there are several important variations. Overall size, capacity for strength and distribution of body weight are some of these differences. However, the woman's potential to conceive and bear children introduces some of the more significant biomechanical differences. These variations will be presented in this section.

Men and Women

Let us first point out some of the physiological differences between men and women. Men are generally 4 inches taller and 29 lbs. heavier than women. The skeletal frame of a man is approximately 8 lbs. heavier than the average woman. Also, the length of arms and legs in proportion to trunk length is more in men than women (Harris, 1977; Katch & McArdle, 1983).

Body fat is another factor in which men and women differ in average amount and distribution. The average percent body fat in men is 15%, versus 27% in women. However, the "essential" body fat in women is higher than in men, and it is suggested that the extra fat is stored about the pelvis and thighs to meet the biological child bearing function. The breast weight was estimated to be no more than 4% of a woman's total body fat in a study which measured women with total percent body fats from 14 to 35% (Katch & McArdle, 1983).

The center of gravity of women is lower than men, and men usually have wider shoulders and heavier upper bodies. When you add pregnancy to the biomechanical structure of a women, further changes occur. The center of gravity stays at about the same height, however it does move forward as the child develops. The lumbar spine is usually also pulled forward into more lordosis, and this is a source of discomfort to many pregnant women.

Pregnancy

Pregnant women gain from approximately 22 to 26 lbs. with most of this gain occurring in the last 2/3 of the pregnancy. The break down of what this weight actually represents is estimated as follows (Edlin & Golanty, 1982):

    7 lbs. fetus
    4 lbs. enlarged uterus/placenta and fluid
    4-8 lbs. blood and extra cellular fluid
    4+ lbs. body fat

There is an understandable loss of balance and coordination, as would be experienced by anyone who gained 22-26 lbs. in nine months. It is now generally accepted that women can continue most of the activities they were used to doing before pregnancy, with some consideration for decreasing the intensity. During heavy exercise there is some shunting of blood from the uterus and fetus to the peripheral muscles (Korcoh, 1981). Starting new activities such as running or skiing is discouraged (Edlin & Golanty, 1982; Katch & McArdle, 1983).

Fatigue is another factor affecting physical activity during pregnancy. The changes in hormone levels and the rapid body changes contribute to the overall feeling of a woman which may make her need more rest. The biomechanical link to this type of fatigue is not established, however, any athlete who is tired and weak for any reason can have performance level changes, as well as a higher risk of injury.

Summary

If all men, women, and children were the same size, body type, strength, and speed, biomechanics could probably be taught in elementary school instead of college. The natural physical variation between people complicates the study of forces acting on and within the human body. This chapter has described many of the considerations relating to injury and these variations. Understanding the importance of anatomical and physiological variations is another important factor in the prevention of injury in sport.

Review Questions

1. Describe how to test for a "functional" or a "structural" scoliosis.

2. Discuss how a mid thoracic scoliosis could cause low back pain.

3. Compare and contrast the implications of a "functional" versus a "true" leg length problem.

4. Discuss the normal biomechanical function of pronation and supination during gait.

5. What are the problems caused by early and excessive pronation?

6. What are the problems associated with excessive supination?

7. At what point in the normal gait cycle does pronation end and supination begin?

8. Discuss the difference between genu varus and valgus.

9. List several reasons for patello-femoral pain.

10. Describe the significance of the Q angle of the knee.

11. What are the two most common structural alignment problems of the hip joint?

12. Briefly discuss the differences between rheumatoid and osteoarthritis.

13. What are some general activity guidelines for a person with rheumatoid arthritis?

14. What joints are usually effected most by rheumatoid arthritis?

15. What joints are usually effected most by osteoarthritis?

16. Describe the major biomechanical change that takes place during pregnancy in relation to center of gravity.

17. List some of the major differences in size and weight distribution between men and women.

18. What are general activity guidelines for pregnant women?

19. What alterations in bone composition occur with aging?

20. What are the implications of these alterations?

21. Name the factors which determine the rate of bone loss.

22. Define osteoporosis and describe its causes.

23. How may one prevent the onset of osteoporosis?

24. How does cartilage composition alter with aging?

25. What happens to ligaments and tendons with aging?

26. What are the consequences of aging muscle?

27. What is the function of the intervertebral disc?

28. What happens to the intervertebral discs with aging?

29. What advice would you give to an aging individual regarding sport or exercise participation?

30. Distinguish between the pressure and traction epiphyses?

31. What is another name for the epiphyseal plate?

32. Where is the weakest portion of the epiphyseal plate?

33. What is the key factor in determining the severity of an epiphyseal fracture?

34. Name and describe an overuse injury specific to young children.

35. Name and describe an articular osteochondroses.

36. What is the mechanism underlying the development of Little Leaguer's Elbow and Osgood-Schlatter's Disease?

37. What precautions should be taken in promoting long distance running in children? weight training?

References

Benton, J. W. (1982). Epiphyseal fracture in sports. The Physician and Sportsmedicine. 10(11), 63-71.

Berkow, R. (Ed.) (1977). Merch Manual (13th ed.). Rahway, NJ: Merch Sharp & Dohme.

Caine, D. J. (1984). Growth plate injury: a threat to young distance runners? The Physician and Sportsmedicine. 12(4), 118-124.

DiStefano, V. J. ( ). How I manage osteochondritis dissecans. The Physician and Sportsmedicine. 14(2), 135-142.

Duda, M. (1986). Prepubescent strength training gains support. The Physician and Sportsmedicine. 14(2), 157-161.

Edlin, G., & Galanty, E. (1982). Health and Wellness. Boston: Science Books International.

Gould, J. A. and Davies, G. J. (1985. Orthopaedic and Sports Physical Therapy, Vol. 2. St Louis: The C. V. Mosby Co.

Harris, D. (1977). Physical sex differences: A matter of degree. NAGWS Research Report, Vol. III. Washington, DC: AAHPER Publication.

Kaplan, F. S. (1987). Osteoporosis: pathophysiology and prevention. Clinical Symposia, 39 (1): 1–32.

Katch, F., & McArdle, W. (1983). Nutrition, Weight Control, and Exercise (2nd ed.). Philadelphia: Lea and Febiger.

Korcoh, M. (1981, July 17). Pregnant jogger: What a record! JAMA Medical News, 246(3), 201.

Larson, R. L., & McMahan, R. O. (1966). The epiphyses and the childhood athlete. Journal of the American Medical Association, 196(7), 99-104.

Marion Laboratories (1984). Osteoporosis: Is It In Your Future?. Kansas City: Marion Laboratories, Inc.

Micheli, L. J., & Micheli, E. R. (1985). Children's running: special risks? Annals of Sports Medicine. 2(2), 61-63.

Morris, J. M. (1973). Biomechanics of the spine. Archives of Surgery, 107:421.

Mow, V. C., Proctor, C. S., and Kelly, M. A. (1989). Biomechanics of articular cartilage. In M. Nordin and V. H. Frankel, Basic Biomechanics of the Musculoskeletal System, (pp. 31–57). Philadelphia: Lea & Febiger.

O'Donoghue, D. H. (1984). Treatment of Injuries to Athletics (4th ed.). Philadelphia: W. B. Saunders.

Panush, R. S. and Martin, R. B. (1984). Exercise and arthritis. Sports Medicine, 4:54–64.

Pappas, A. M. (1983). Epiphyseal injuries in sports. The Physician and Sportsmedicine. 11(6), 140-148.

Pappas, A. M. (1989). Osteochondroses: diseases of growth cen Physician and Sportsmedicine. 17(6), 51-62.

Peterson, C. A., & Peterson, H. A. ( ). Analysis of the incidence of injurie to the epiphyseal growth plate. The Journal of Trauma. 12(4), 275-281.

Radin, E. L. and Martin, R. B. (1984). Biomechanics of joint deterioration and osteoarthritis. In C. L. Nelson and Dwyer, A. P. (Eds.), The Aging Musculoskeletal System: Physiological and Pathological Problems, (pp. 127–134). New York: The Collamore Press.

Rogers, S. L. (1982). The Aging Skeleton: Aspects of Human Bone Involution. Springfield, IL: Charles C. Thomas Publisher.

Salter, R. (1970). Textbook of Disorders and Injuries to the Musculoskeletal System. Baltimore: Williams and Williams.

Salter, R. B., & Harris, W. R. (1963). Injuries involving the epiphyseal plate. Journal of Bone and Joint Surgery. 45A(3), 587-622.

Speer, D. P., & Braun, K. (1985). The biomechanical basis of growth plate injuries. The Physician and Sportsmedicine. 13(7), 72-78.

Thomas, C. L. (Ed.). (1978). Taber's Cyclopedic Medical Dictionary (13th ed.). Philadelphia: F. A. Davis Company.

7

fic Injury Prevention Methods

Wolff's Law
> Bone
> Cartilage
> Ligaments and Tendons
> Muscle

Stretching to Prevent Musculoskeletal Injuries

Preparticipation Exam
> Screening
> Pre-existing Conditions

New Prevention Ideas
> Profiling

Protective Equipment
> Biomechanical Concepts
> Situations for which Protection is Needed
> Sports Equipment Certification Committees
> Protective Devices

Summary

Review Questions

References

Suggested Readings

There are so many factors which contribute to the prevention of sports injuries that it is tempting to be excessively general in the presentation of this material. A comprehensive approach to injury prevention is obviously best, and there are many other prevention factors than can be presented here. However, the purpose of this text is to present biomechanical information and considerations for the reader to add to the total prevention program for the maximum prevention results. In this chapter there will be considerable attention given to the biomechanical aspects of the training and de-training effect on specific connective tissues. And, there will be some attention given to the pre-participation examination and physical assessment. The benefits of stretching and attaining normal range of motion also will be presented.

Wolff's Law

Wolff's Law basically states that bone remodels in response to the stress or lack of stress which is applied to it. (See also Chapter 3.) The response is that bone tissue grows and is strengthened in environments of additional stress. They demineralize and become weaker in conditions of normal stress deprivation. This law is now appreciated for its universal truth as it is related to other systems and tissues of the body as well as the mind. It does not, however, extend to the limit indicated in a quote observed on a graduate student's bulletin board; "That which does not kill you makes you stronger." There are negative effects of overuse on the musculoskeletal system, just like everything else.

Well designed training programs do strengthen the musculoskeletal system. However, the rate of change in the different tissues due to the training effort is quite variable. This variability, and the lack of understanding, leads to many preventable injuries. As the training effect on each tissue is presented, try to get some sense of the timing of its response.

Bone

In a study using swine, it was found that after 12 months of training, there was an increase of 17 percent in cortical thickness and 23 percent of cortical cross section area. Individual 4 millimeter wide strips of the bone were found to have the same force point bending test results. Therefore, it was concluded that although the per unit bone material is the same in strength, there is more bone material present after the training to withstand applied stress (Woo et al., 1981). However, the appropriate amount of training was addressed more specifically in a study done on growing mice. This study found that growing mice who ran 80 minutes per day at 18 m/min. for 12 weeks had longer and heavier femurs than the non-exercising controls. The second sample of growing mice were subjected to two different conditions of either increasing the duration to 21 weeks instead of 12, or increasing the daily running time to 120 minutes instead of the 80 minutes. The femurs were then found to be both shorter and lighter (Booth & Gould, 1975). So much for "more is better."

A functional adaptation of bone was reported in a study involving swine. The swine were initially measured for total circumference, cortical thickness, and compressive strain on the radius. Then one group of swine underwent a unilateral removal of the diaphysis of the ulna. The compressive strain on the remaining radius immediately increased from 2 to 2-1/2 times the pre-ulnarectomy measurements. After three months, the radius on the side of the ulnarectomy responded to the additional stress by increasing the circumference and cross sectional bone measurements to nearly the same value of the radius and ulna together on the normal side (Goodship et al., 1979).

Human studies also support this response to additional functional stress. X-rays have shown an increase in the cortical thickness of the playing side arm in tennis players. Also, bone-mineral content was shown to be 20% greater in a group of cross country runners (Woo et al., 1981). As far back as in 1924, Kohlrausch determined that famous bass viola players had abnormally large left as compared to right hands.

These studies all support the idea that appropriate levels of stress on bones will increase their size and strength. What remains to be determined is how the rate of growth of bone material compares with other connective tissues of the body. From the studies reviewed, the functional adaptation study seems to give the best evidence. Remember the amount of time it took for the radii in the swine to assume the size and strength of the radii and ulna together on the normal side was three months (Goodship et al., 1979).

De-training effects on bone tissue also is well known. Paraplegics and muscular dystrophy victims have shown bone loss on x-rays after periods of non-weight bearing. Whedon and Shorr studied the effects of non-weight bearing on acute polio victims and found that after 3 months x-rays could detect osteoporosis (Booth & Gould, 1975). Bed rest studies on healthy subjects also support evidence that bone material is lost during disuse.

Booth and Gould (1975), in their reports on the training and de-training effects on connective tissue, make an additional point that muscle weight and bone weight correlate highly for both training and de-training. They also predict that heavy resistance training, instead of low level endurance training, will lead to greater bone hypertrophy.

Cartilage

The body of research concerned with the effects of training and de-training on articular cartilage is considerably less than the research on bone. However, several cartilage studies have been done on rabbits. The research shows that rabbits that were either exercised or had large pen areas for running, had significantly greater articular cartilage thickness after 16 weeks than did small cage groups of rabbits (Booth & Gould, 1975). These authors reported that both the cellular and intercellular components of the cartilage had increases in thickness. The increase of the intercellular components was most dramatic (4X that of cellular components).

Other studies on injured articular cartilage suggest that continuous passive motion seems to stimulate the best environment for articular cartilage repair when compared with intermittent motion or immobilization (Knortz, 1986). The authors of this research speculate that the continuous motion assists with the healing by continually bathing the area with synonial fluid which improves the nutritional environment.

As was presented in Chapter 6, individuals with osteo and rheumatoid arthritis need the medical management of physicians and supervision by physical therapists to regulate the correct level of activity for them.

Ligaments and Tendons

As with other musculoskeletal tissue, ligaments and tendons do strengthen with activity and become weaker with inactivity (Booth & Gould, 1975; Cabaud et al., 1980; Knortz, 1986; Laros et al., 1971; Noyes et al., 1974). What is less understood is how long it takes for these changes to take place. The tensile strength of patella tendons in exercised mice increased in 3 weeks, and chemical changes were observable in as few as 15 days in mice (Booth & Gould, 1975). In a study of rats, exercise for 8 weeks showed significant increase in anterior cruciate ligament strength. Another important note about this study is that it was found that rats exercised daily for 30 minutes showed greater strength increases than those who exercised every other day for 60 minutes. (Cabaud et al., 1980). This is not to say that the frequency or duration of exercise noted here is applicable to humans, but it does point out that animals do respond differently to various exercise programs.

Experiments on ligament insertions of dogs involved the three conditions of active, inactive, and casted. As you might expect by now, the results were consistent with previous studies which support the relationship of greater strength with conditions of greater opportunity for activity. This study showed changes in strength after 6 weeks (Laros et al., 1971).

Primate studies regarding ligament strength demonstrated that there was a decrease in both maximum load and energy absorbed after 8 weeks of immobilization of the anterior cruciate. At the end of 20 weeks of resumed activity after the 8 weeks of immobilization, in another group of primates, there was only partial return of ligament strength (Noyes et al., 1974).

It is further suggested that ligaments that are injured and then repaired are stronger after 6 weeks when they are not immobilized as compared with animals that were casted for six weeks (Booth & Gould, 1975).

From these studies it would seem that it takes from 6 to 8 weeks to see improvement in ligament and tendon strength due to training. Likewise, it would seem to take about that long to see a decrease in strength after immobilization. Returning to strength levels after immobilization, however, appears to take a disproportionately longer period of time.

Muscle

The training of muscle tissue has more dramatic results than does the training of other connective tissue. Some authors have reported that there are recordable chemical changes in as little as 2-3 days (Booth & Gould, 1975). Resistance training may result in strength gains of 4% per week or approximately 15% per month (Wescott, 1982).

There are numerous types of training programs, such as isometric, isotonic, isokinetic, and plyometrics, to name a few. The result of each program is different in relation to the speed of the strength gains, amount of hypertrophy, or the specific speed and point in the range of motion that the increase in strength is most evident. In fact, each person's training program could be just as individual and personal as the way you wear your clothes and style your hair.

The difference in muscle response to training between men and women is also interesting to consider. A study involving untrained subjects, using approximately 50 men and 50 women determined the following (Katch & McArdle, 1983):

1) The pre-training strength levels were higher in men than women by 28% and 26% for the upper and lower body respectively.

2) When comparing body weight to strength, the men and women were nearly equal.

3) After 10 weeks of weight training, both the men and women increased their strength by approximately 30%.

4) After the 10 weeks of weight training, the women had surpassed the pre-weight training strength level of the men.

5) The women did not show the same amount of hypertrophy that the men did after training.

Muscle tissue is more vascular than is any of the other connective tissue reported on in this chapter. This accounts for its more rapid increase in strength and adaptation to stress levels. Likewise, the de-training and immobilization effects on muscle are drastic. It is generally accepted in rehabilitation that strict bed rest will cause 3% strength loss per day. Immobilization by casting will cause significant atrophy of muscle tissue, and a commensurate amount of weakness and loss of function. If you have ever seen or experienced what a leg or arm looks like when the cast is first removed after six weeks of immobilization, you can appreciate the term "atrophy."

A body that is either untrained or highly trained may not be as susceptible to injury as one in transition if the level of stress is proportionate. There is a state of homeostasis that will eventually be reached as all systems accommodate. But, from the information presented in this chapter, it is easy to see that there is a potential for a wide disparity in the strength levels of the various types of connective tissue, especially during training. The untrained individual and the well trained individual have both reached a balance in the strength of their tissues. In other words, the muscle cannot pull too hard for the strength of the tendon. Fortunately, the body has built in safety factors for its structure. An example of this is the case of the training weight lifter who ruptured his patellar tendon while lifting a 175 Kg. weight. The tension on the tendon at the time of the rupture was computed to be 17 times his body weight (Curwin & Standish, 1984). Normal and functional forces are not that high. Also, the weight lifter had trained his muscles beyond the strength of the tendon.

Still, there are a lot of submaximal stress levels which put our musculoskel-etal systems into the strain and plastic region of their stress/strain curves. The repeated application of these levels of force will begin to break down and irritate the system and result in injury. During a training program, it would be valuable to keep the various connective tissues together in regard to their increase in strength. Since this is really not possible, then we need to be aware of which tissues are ahead, and which are lagging behind.

The present literature does not lay this out very neatly for us so we can have objective data upon which to base our opinion and make our decisions. For example, it would be helpful to have a time line chart which showed the expected strength increase of each specific tissue at intervals in the training program. If you attempted to do this by interpolating existing literature results, it could look like Figure 7.1.

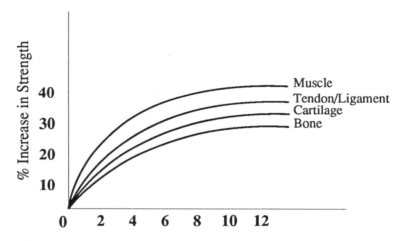

Figure 7.1.
Postulated strength increase curve. Training Time in Months

Remember that this model is only postulated and not supported by specific research. If a model was proposed for the same tissues regarding a loss of strength due to de-training, one could expect the inverse relationship to occur (see Figure 7.2).

What these figures suggest is that during a training program, there is a risk of injuring the tissue which does not respond to training as quickly. For example, if after two months, the muscle has increased in strength by 25% and the ligaments and tendons have only increased by 15%, there is a greater chance of ligament or tendon injury. Likewise, if after 6 months of training, the muscles and tendon/ligaments have increased their strength by 35 and 25% respectively, and bone strength had only increased by 15%, there is a greater chance for a stress fracture.

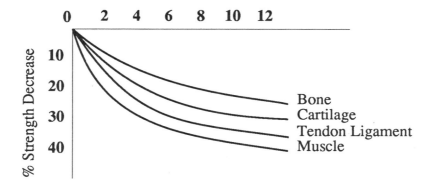

Figure 7.2.

Postulated strength decrease curve.   Training Time in Months

This is probably why slow progressive programs cause so many fewer injuries than do rapidly accelerated training programs. The slower progressed programs allow for more harmony between the various types of connective tissue.

Another way to visualize the effects of training and de-training is to examine the graph below. (See figure 7.3) You will see that for any tissue the response to stimulus is that for any bout of exercise or individual exposure force, the stress of the tissue is pushed above the normal baseline. Likewise, decrease in activity and de-training causes the stress on an individual tissue to drop below its baseline.

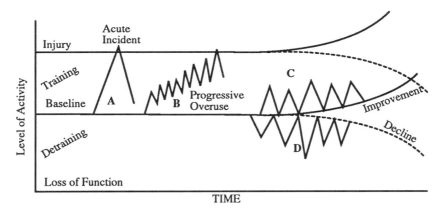

Figure 7.3.

Postulated effects of training and detraining. A) Acute injury B) Overuse injury C) The training effect improves baseline condition and increases protection from injury D) The detraining effect lowers baseline condition and decreases protection from injury

Acute onsets of injury push the stress level to the range of failure in one single event. (See "A") Whereas, overuse syndromes require a succession of stress bouts, but the tissue is not given sufficient time to recover to the baseline before another stimulus is applied driving the stress level higher. (See "B")

Training with appropriate progression, as in "C", will raise the baseline of tissue strength. This would account for the "training effect" that athletes are looking for. The de-training effect is also experienced with a resultant decrease in the baseline as is shown by line "D".

Stretching to Prevent Musculoskeletal Injuries

Experts in the field are of the opinion that empirical evidence supports stretching as a means of preventing injuries, even though the scientific evidence is not there. This is no surprise since: (1) all factors affecting range of motion about a joint cannot be controlled; (2) relating injury to a lack of flexibility is difficult to assess, and (3) the use of human subjects poses a very ethical problem.

Intuitively, one would surmise that stretching does improve range of motion. Consider the connective tissues of the body: tendons, ligaments, joint capsules, aponeuroses, and fascia. They are made up primarily of collagen, a fibrous protein with high tensile forces (See Chapter 3). These collagenous tissues also are considered to be viscoelastic. That is, they contain both elastic and plastic elements. When a tissue is stretched, the elastic elements allow the tissue to return to its original shape and condition when the load is released. The plastic elements, on the other hand, cause a certain amount of permanent deformation to occur. How much permanent deformation occurs depends upon how the stretching is performed and under what conditions.

Sapega, et al. (1981) addressed the question of how stretching should be performed and under what conditions. They based their conclusions upon the work of Warren et. al. (1971) at the University of Washington who worked on rat tendons. The interpretation of the results led to the conclusion that a stretching program results in some permanent deformation of the connective tissue. It was further suggested that this goal might be a more desirable goal for therapeutic conditions, but that it could apply also to non-injured persons participating in an exercise or sport program.

It was suggested that gentle, static-like stretching of long duration should be done for maximum effectiveness. A key point being emphasized was the effectiveness of an elevated tissue temperature prior to the stretching. Physiologically speaking, elevated tissue temperatures: (1) promote more efficient use of substrates that are crucial for providing necessary energy for activity; (2) promote more efficient muscle contraction; (3) enhance the function of the nervous system; and (4) improve the flow of blood to the skeletal muscles. Further elevated tissue temperatures cause greater muscle elasticity, thus making the muscle less susceptible to injury or damage (Shellock and Prentice, 1985). A caution was issued to exercisers who used stretching exercises. A "warm-up" activity such as brisk walking or light jogging should be performed before actual stretching was begun.

In a more recent study by Safran, et. al. (1988), an attempt was made to provide further support for the practice of "warming up" prior to an exercise task. Their subjects were rabbits whose tibialis anterior, extensor digitorum longus, and flexor digitorum longus were studied under two conditions, a pre-conditioned isometric contraction where muscle temperature was elevated and a non-isometric contraction condition. Tears in the isometrically preconditioned muscle were compared to tears in controlled muscle by examining: (1) force to failure; (2) change of length required to tear the muscle; (3) site of failure; and (4) length-tension deformation. Two findings of significance were: (1) a greater force was needed to tear the muscle under pre-conditioned (warmed) muscle; and (2) an increase in length was needed to tear the preconditioned muscle. It was concluded that under pre-conditioning less tension was placed on the metatarsal joint resulting in a reduced incidence of injury.

Dominguez, an orthopaedist in sports medicine, has another opinion concerning stretching. His conclusions regarding stretching are based on observation. He advocates stretching exercises be performed by those individuals who are engaging in dynamic range of motion activities such as throwing or sprinting. The more explosive or powerful the move, the more "stretching" should be done. Therefore, in his opinion, joggers need not stretch before running because it is not considered a dynamic activity. His evidence was based on strain injuries he has seen in runners. (Roundtable, 1984).

Although there is not overwhelming scientific evidence to say that stretching can prevent injury by improving range of motion, empirical evidence weighs heavily in favor of a stretching program prior to an exercise task. These are some general guidelines:

1. Tissue temperature should be elevated to improve the viscoelasticity of the tissues.
2. A slow stretch should be used.
3. The stretch should be of long duration.

---

4. The stretch should be of low force.
5. Stretching should be done before performing dynamic movements.

Pre-Participation Examination

One essential element for any prevention program is the pre-participation examination or PPE. As of this writing, there are thirty-five states in the United States which require PPEs annually for organized competition. Thirty-six states provide a form for the examination which includes medical history questions and lists of organ systems for the examining physician (Feinstein et al., 1988). The American Medical Association has approved a form for the examination, and they have established a list of recommended contraindications for participation. The American Academy of Pediatrics has also been very active in providing guidelines and recommendations for the administering of PPEs.

Screening

One specific example of a pre-participation examination for participation in an exercise program takes the form of "screening levels" (Physical Fitness Specialist Course Manual, Institute for Aerobics Research, 1979). The individual participant is started at level 1 and based on the results of preliminary tests, he or she moves to either the High Risk group or Level 2. The screening levels program works like a decision tree; the individual is moved through appropriate but not excessive testing. Those who fall into the High Risk group after level 1 screening, undergo closer scrutiny with a medical exam and a stress test. Those who pass level one and go directly to level two, have an aerobic test to determine if they need to go back to the High Risk group, begin an easier starter program, or move on to Level 3. Only after an individual successfully passes through the field tests of level 3 can he or she begin the aerobic training program. See figure (7.4) for a diagram of the screening level program and a list of High Risk Indicators.

Pre-Existing Conditions.

Examples of conditions which limit activity include having only one kidney, or one eye, or being hemophiliac. These problems are relatively rare when compared to the problems of the musculoskeletal system which are so important to physical

---

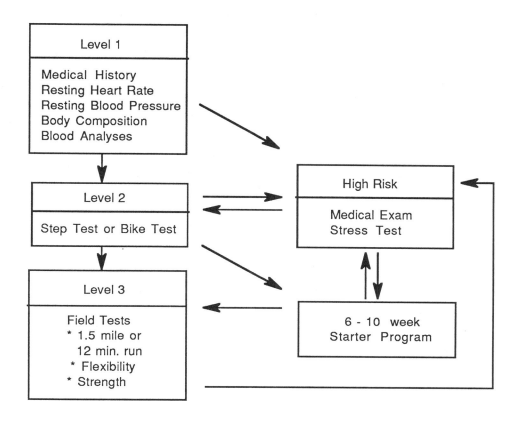

Figure 7.4.
Screening level program and high risk indicators. (Adapted with permission from Physical Fitness Specialist Course, Institute for Aerobics Research, 1979.)

activity. The musculoskeletal system should be thoroughly evaluated for variances which would lead to injury. The variances covered in Chapter 6 such as scoliosis, arthritis, and leg length discrepancies should be evaluated prior to participation. It also is important to track the progression or correction of these conditions as the athlete grows and develops.

An important part of the musculoskeletal examination is the injury history. All previous injuries such as sprains, strains, and fractures should be specifically evaluated to insure the sport or exercise participant has regained full range of motion, strength, and proprioceptive function of the injured part. Additional isokinetic strength testing and goniometry may be required to accurately evaluate the status of the previously injured person.

If there is a deficiency noted, recommendations for alleviation of the problem need to be outlined for the participant. A home stretching or strengthening program, or direct rehabilitation in the training room or physical therapy clinic, or both, may be required. On some more serious problems, such as ligament damage, a referral to an orthopedic specialist may be required to adequately determine if the individual should participate. Specific protective equipment or taping may be required for the prevention of a reinjury. Motivating the participant to comply with the restrictions and recommendations is of key importance to insure the most benefit from injury prevention efforts.

New Prevention Ideas

In the past few years, there has been an increase in prevention efforts, and likewise a few new ideas. One of these ideas is to use maturation as a guide to competition level instead of age or size. We have all observed the disparity in maturation of some children in school. Besides the obvious changes in secondary sex characteristics, there are significant differences in strength, power, and bone density, to name a few.

The problems inherent in a maturity classification are many. The observation by a physician is still very subjective, and growth plate closure studies are not practical due to the cost as well as the unnecessary exposure to radiation. Another problem with maturation assessments is the potential additional stress on the developing young person, who is already going through a lot of psychological and emotional adjustments without a public judgment being made on their stage of physical maturity.

Training

There are many examples of technique training in sports that help prevent injury such as throwing a curve ball correctly to protect the elbow and keeping your head up during blocking in football. A new example of an injury prevention technique involves protection of the anterior cruciate ligament. The technique involves avoiding the potentially dangerous extension position of the knee under conditions of high mechanical knee forces. The activities of stopping and landing from a jump are done in a two or three step, bent knee fashion instead of in full or near full extension. Sharp turns or cutting is done in the bent knee position with more force applied by the inside leg. The corner is made in a slightly rounded fashion while accelerating, instead of forcefully planting the outside leg in full extension to get a sharp diagonal cut. The acceptance of these technique changes by older and advanced athletes is difficult, however the acceptance by school age children is promising.

Profiling

Another relatively new idea is called "profiling." This involves the attempted prediction of injury based on body variances and previous injuries (Moore, 1981; Sapega & Nicholas, 1981). This program is used in some professional programs where there is the advantage of several years of injury history, as well as state of the art facilities, equipment, and medical supervision. One research program which was reported in 1978 attempted to predict the injuries of young athletes. In this study 2,817 athletes were evaluated for joint flexibility and no statistical relationship could be established between injury frequency and preexisting joint laxity or tightness (Jackson et al., 1978).

In recent years, some athletes who have been disqualified from participation have challenged it through legal means. In this situation, it is imperative that the athlete, or their parents if underaged, be informed as to the specific risks and potential harm that may be present.

Protective Equipment

Practically speaking, protective equipment should be worn or used to reduce the risk of injury by protecting body parts or preventing further injury from occurring. Biomechanically speaking, protective equipment is needed to: (1) absorb kinetic energy; (2) deflect blows or objects; and (3) stabilize a body part.

Biomechanical Concepts

Four biomechanical concepts describe the principle behind the design of sports equipment. They are pressure, impulse- momentum, work-kinetic energy, and friction.

Pressure. Recalling from Chapter 1, pressure was defined as the ratio of force to area. If an impact is to be dissipated, the force must be spread over a large area. For example, protective padding such as that found on the thigh of a football player would protect him from a blow.

Impulse-Momentum. Force over time results in a change in momentum. If that force can be absorbed over time, the change in momentum can act in favor of the individual. For instance, a boxer who can "roll with the punch" may avoid a knockout.

Work-Kinetic Energy. Work depends on a force being applied over a distance. Kinetic energy depends upon the mass of the object and the velocity with which it is moving. By rearranging the work and kinetic energy formulas, one can observe that the force of an impact is proportional to the kinetic energy, and inversely proportional to the distance over which it is applied

$$F = \frac{1/2 \ m \ v^2}{d}$$

In catching a hard thrown ball, the arms are drawn to the chest to absorb the force over a distance.

Friction. Friction is the force between two surfaces which enhances or inhibits motion. A glove is worn in gymnastics to reduce the friction between skin and equipment, thereby, preventing blisters.

Situations For Which Protection is Needed

The first thing that comes to one's mind when discussing equipment is protection for impact/collision situations. This is not too surprising when considering the consequences of receiving a blow. Serious injuries can occur, especially if the impact situations are to the head. However, there are other situations in which impacts may cause injuries. The repeated impact of the foot on the ground during running may cause an injury such as a stress fracture if proper shoes are not worn.

Implements also may cause blows to the body. Broken bats, a racquet that slips from a hand, or a fencing foil are potential sources for injury. Objects moving at high speeds pose a risk for injury. A wild pitch in baseball, a racquetball off the wall, or a hockey puck are examples.

Playing surface material may make a difference in injury risks. Tartan surface material, concrete, asphalt, and wooden surfaces all contribute to the possibility of injury. For instance, turf toe is a potential injury on tartan surfaces in football, overuse injuries in running on concrete surfaces, or scrapes and burns from falling on asphalt or wood surfaces.

Sports Equipment Certification Committees

Two organizations actively are involved in setting standards for safety in the use of sport equipment. They are the American Society for Testing and Materials (ASTM) and the National Operating Committee on Standards for Athletic Equipment (NOCSAE).

ASTM. This organization was founded in 1898 for "the development of standards on characteristics and performance of materials, products, systems, and services; and the promotion of related knowledge." (Annual Book of ASTM Standards, 1984) In 1969, the Committee on Sports Equipment and Facilities was established to establish "standardization of specifications, test methods, and recommended practices for sports equipment and facilities to minimize injury, and promotion of knowledge as it relates to protective equipment standards."

NOCSAE. This committee was established in 1969 as the result of the increasing numbers of participants injured while actively engaged in sport activities. Their first efforts were in the area of football where equipment standards were sought for the manufacture and use of helmets. They later directed their research efforts toward neck injuries in football and hockey, faceguard attachments, thigh pads, and baseball/softball batting helmets.

The NOCSAE Football Helmet Standard was published in 1973, and the Baseball Helmet Standard followed in 1981. Every player playing under NCAA or National Federation rules in either sport is required to wear a NOCSAE approved helmet. The helmets can be identified by the seal on the helmet which reads "meets NOCSAE Standard".

Protective Devices

Table 7.1 demonstrates typical protective devices for various parts of the body. Examples of sports in which the devices may be used also are given.

Table 7.1. Protective Devices Used in Sports Activities.

Body Part	Protective Device	Sport
Head	Helmets	Football, baseball, hockey, cycling
Face	Masks	Baseball, hockey
Mouth	Guards	Football, boxing
Ear	Guards	Wrestling, boxing
Eye	Guards	Racquetball, handball
Chest	Pad	Football, baseball
Breast	Bra	Jogging
Genitals	Cup	Baseball
Shoulder	Pads	Football
Elbow, wrist	Pads	Football
Hand	Gloves	Baseball, softball, handball
Hip	Pads	Football
Knee, ankle	Pads, brace	Volleyball, football
Foot	Shoes	Any sport

Anyone who participates in a sport or exercise activity assumes some risk for injury. Protective equipment is not a guarantee for an injury-free activity session. Designing equipment for ultimate protection is nearly impossible. Movement, visual field, or comfort may be compromised if this were to be done. Other problems in designing the ultimate protection are universal fit, weight, temperature control, and long-lasting materials. Perhaps the greatest limitation to the perfect design is the lack of information regarding human tolerance levels to forces.

Summary

The prevention of injury is a realistic goal for anyone participating in a sport or activity. However, the specific methods employed to meet this goal are many and varied. Consider the example of a person who decides to start a running program for health and aerobic fitness. A pre-participation physical may be advisable depending on age. Once the physical is "passed," there are many other considerations. This chapter has provided information to use for the prevention of injury through a knowledge of the physical status of the participant as well as knowledge of several other factors. Below is a summary list of these considerations for the runner.

1. participant's exercise history

2. participant's current fitness level

3. participant's previous injuries/illnesses

4. participant's fitness or running goals

5. participant's biomechanics (i.e., excessive pronator/ supinator, etc.

6. shoes

7. running surface and grade

8. desired distance or time

9. weather

Review Questions

1. Briefly describe Wolff's Law.

2. Explain the differences in the training response of the major musculoskeletal tissues.

3. Discuss the effect of de-training and bed rest on musculoskeletal tissue and describe what you might expect regarding the rate and order at which the various tissues are affected.

4. Describe the training effects on muscle for men and women.

5. What are the relationships of strength levels before and after a resistance training program in men and women?

6. Discuss the benefits of good pre-participation examinations.

7. Describe some efforts and problems with predicting injury in athletes.

8. Reflect on your own experience with pre-participation examinations and report on their quality and prevention potential.

9. What are the benefits of stretching or warming up before participating in a sport or exercise?

10. Define viscoelastic. How does it play a role in connective tissue stretching?

11. Should stretching prior to engaging in a sport or exercise activity always be done?

12. What guidelines should you follow in stretching or warming up before participating in a sport or exercise activity?

13. For what purposes should protective equipment be worn?

14. How do the following biomechanical concepts relate to injury prevention by wearing protective equipment: pressure, impulse-momentum, work-kinetic energy, friction?

15. Name at least three mechanisms of injury for which protection is needed?

16. What is the purpose of ASTM? NOCSAE?

17. Name a sport and then identify the protective equipment which should be worn for that sport.

References

American Society for Testing and Materials. (1984). Annual Book of ASTM Testing and Materials. 15.07, iii.

Booth, F., & Gould, E. (1975). Effects of training and disuse on connective tissues. Exercise and Sports Science Reviews, Vol. 3. New York: Academic Press, Inc.

Cabaud, H., Chatty, A., Gildengorin, V., & Feltman, R. (1980). Exercise effects on the strength of the rat anterior cruciate ligament. The American Journal of Sports Medicine, 8(2), 79-84.

Curwin, S. & Standish, W. (1984). Tendonitis: Its Etiology and Treatment. Lexington: D. C. Heath and co.

Feinstein, R., Soilean, E., & Daniel, W. (1988, May). A national survey of participation physical examination requirements. The Physician and Sportsmedicine, 16(5), 45-51.

Goodship, A., Lanyuon, L., & McFie, H. (1979, June). Functional adaptation of bone to increased stress. Journal of Bone and Joint Surgery, 61-A(4), 539-548.

Hoerner, E. F., & Vinger, P. F. (Eds.). (1986). Sports Injuries: The Unthwarted Epidemic. Littleton, MA: PSG Publishing Company, Inc.

Jackson, D., Jarrett, H., Bailey, D., Kausek, J., Swanson, J., & Powell, J. (1978, January). Injury prediction in the young athlete: A preliminary record. The American Journal of Sports Medicine, 6(1), 6-14.

Katch, F. & McCardle, W. (1983). Nutrition, Weight Control, and Exercise (2nd ed.) Philadelphia: Lea & Febiger.

Knortz, K. (1986, March). Effects of immobilization and exercise on connective tissue. P. T. Forum, 5(12), 1-4.

Laros, G., Tipton, G., & Cooper, K. (1971, March). Influence of physical activity on ligament insertions in the knees of dogs. Journal of Bone and Joint Surgery, 53-A(2), 79-84.

Moore, M. (1981, February). Risk profiling of pro football players. The Physician and Sports Medicine, 9(2), 131-135.

National Operating Committee on Standards for Athletic Equipment. Unpublished paper.

Noyes, F., DeLucas, J., & Torvih, P. (1974, March). Biomechanics of anterior cruciate ligament failure: An analysis of strain-rate sensitivity and mechanism of failure in primates. Journal of Bone and Joint Surgery, 56-A(2), 236-245.

Noyes, F., Torvih, P., Hyde, W., & DeLucas, J. (1974, October). Biomechanics of ligament failures. Journal of Bone and Joint Surgery, 56-A(7), 1406-1417.

Physical Fitness Specialist Course Manual. (1979). Dallas, TX: Institute for Aerobics Research.

Roundtable. (1984). Flexibility. National Strength and Conditioning Association Journal 6(4), 12-22, 71-73.

Safran, M. R., et. al. (1988). The role of warmup in muscular injury prevention. The American Journal of Sports Medicine, 16(2), 123-128.

Sapega, A. A. & Nicholas, J. A. The clinical use of musculoskeletal profiling in orthopedic sports medicine. The Physician and Sports Medicine, 9 (4), 80–88.

Sapega, A. A., et. al. (1981). Biophysical factors in range-of- motion exercise. The Physician and Sportsmedicine 9(12), 57-65.

Shellock, F. G. and W. E. Prentice. (1985). Warming-up and stretching for improved physical performance and prevention of sports-related injuries. Sports Medicine 2, 267-278.

Shyne, K. (1982). Richard H. Dominguez, MD: To stretch or not to stretch?. The Physician and Sportsmedicine. 10(9), 337-340.

Warren, C. G., Lehman, J. F., and J. N. Kobianski. (1971). Elongation of rat tendon: effect of load and temperature. Archives of Physical Medicine and Rehabilitation 51, 465-474.

Westcott, W. L. (1982). Strength Fitness. Boston: Allyn and Bacon Inc.

Wilford, H. N., et. al. (1966). Evaluation of warm-up for improvement in flexibility. The American Journal of Sports Medicine 14(6), 316-319.

Woo, S., Kevi, S., Amiel, D., Gomez, M., Wilson, C., White, F., & Akeson, W. (1981, June). The effect of prolonged physical training of the properties of long bone: A study of Wolff's Law. Journal of Bone and Joint Surgery, 67-A(5), 780-786.

Suggested Readings

Connective Tissue (general)

1. Beyer, R. (1983). Regulation of C.T. Metabolism in Aging and Exercise: A Review, Psychological Effects of Exercise.

2. Nicholas, J. A., & Hershman, B. (1986). The Lower Extremity and Spine in Sports Medicine, vol. 1. St. Louis, MO: C. V. Mosby Company.

Bone

3. Anderson, Milin, & Crackel. (1971, June). Effects of Exercise on Mineral and Organic Bone Turnover in Swine. Journal of Applied Physiology, 30(6).

Cartilage

4. Gould. Orthopedic and Sports Physical Therapy, Chapter 4, p. 107.

Tendon

5. Ciullo, J. V., & Zarius, B. (1983). Biomechanics of the Musculotendionous UniJt: Relation to Athletic Performance and Injury. Clinical Sports Medicine, 2, 71.

6. Elliott, D. H. (1967). The Mechanical Properties of Tendon in Relation to Muscular Strength. Annals of Physical Medicine, 9, 127J.

Ligament

7. Laros, Tipton, & Cooper. Influence of Physical Activity on Ligament Insertions in the Knees of Dogs. Journal of Bone and Joint Surgery, 53-A(2).

8. Zukerman, & Stull. (1973). Ligamentous Separation Force in Rats as Influenced by Training, De-Training, and Cage Restriction. Medicine and Science in Sports, 5(1).

Overtraining

9. The Limits to Training. (1980, June). Physician and Sportsmedicine, 8(6).

10. Stamford. (1983, October). Overtraining and Cardio-Vascular Fitness. Physician and Sportsmedicine, 11(10).

8

The Rehabilitation Process

Introduction

As was noted in Chapter 1, a major prevention task is to prevent the recurrence or extension of an injury. In order to adequately do this, some knowledge of the rehabilitation involved in sports and activity injuries is beneficial.

Goals of Rehabilitation

Rehabilitation of an injury is a special process which ideally should have the following goals:

1. Return to original sport or exercise program as soon as possible.

2. Prevent extending the injury during rehab or from returning too early to the sport or exercise program.

3. Maintain conditioning level as high as possible while resting and conditioning the injured area.

4. Improve in some physical aspect of your game or sport that does not stress the injured area.

5. Utilize time of rehab for achieving a psychological break from the training program.

6. Accomplish the skill training, strengthening, or range of motion to help prevent further injury.

Some participants might look at this list and say... "If I could count on meeting these goals, then I should get hurt more often." Of course this is being facetious. However, there are positive factors which should not be overlooked regarding well designed rehabilitation programs.

The first guideline to a successful rehabilitation program is to initially avoid repeats of the injury-causing mechanical force. This may sound absurd, but sadly this advice is not always heeded. Everyone hates to slow down, change their techniques, abstain from their training, or participate in an alternate activity. The key to being happy is in knowing that you are doing all that you can to meet the goals of the rehabilitation program as stated above.

Working Around the Injury

Since time is very important, it is essential to rest the injured part while still working on some aspect of the training program. You literally have to "work around the problem." An example of this would be a pitcher with a rotator cuff strain. Although the major skill of his game, throwing the ball, requires rest, he can still work on fielding ground balls, running and aerobic training, muscle strengthening (except for the arm), studying hitters in his league, or situational visualization. Meanwhile, he may be going to the training room, or physical therapy clinic, or doing his own home treatment with ice, stretch, and allowable resistance programs.

Aerobic Training

Aerobic training during a musculoskeletal injury is very important. It is well known that injuries happen more frequently when the person is fatigued. Aerobic conditioning can help prevent injury once a person returns to activity. Besides the physical benefits, aerobic training is a good diversion for the participant to help decrease anxiety or depression about his/her inability to fully participate.

Making Good Use of Rehabilitation Time

The psychological benefits of a break in the training program have been seen in some people. You may know of baseball players who always seem to go on a hitting streak just after returning to the lineup from an injury. Some swimmers also get their best times shortly after an injury break. This has something to do with being psychologically and physically rested or "fresh."

It is sometimes suggested that technique work can be done during an injury; however, it must be clearly understood that the injured part cannot be involved in the specific motion. For example, a golfer with low back pain may not be able to work on her putting if she experiences any back pain during the putting motion. Sometimes poor habits are learned when trying to work around an injury if it changes your posture, or the biomechanics of the skill. Then when the original problem has resolved and the person returns to full activity, they are truly worse off than before the injury.

As was alluded to in an earlier example, the injured person may make best use of his/her time doing non-physical training activities such as working on concentration, eye discipline drills, or visualizations. Again, this can take the place of some of the normal practice or training time that the injured person is unable to do during part of the rehabilitation process.

When speaking specifically about the injured part, it is important to know when to resume some activity and how to progress. The attending physician may have some specific directions about this, but sometimes it is determined by the injured person's own functional or strength level. For example, after an anterior cruciate ligament repair of the knee, there is usually a specific set of progression guidelines followed by the therapist or trainer. The guidelines cover specifics such as how much weight bearing is allowed, range of motion limitations (active and passive), and which muscle groups may be resisted (how much and when). Toward the end of the rehabilitation process, the protocol becomes much less dependent on a predetermined time or weight limitation, and more dependent on the patient's own progress in balancing strength from the involved leg to the normal leg. Many orthopedic surgeons require the patient to return to 80 or 90% of the strength of the normal side in order to return to even limited activity.

How Much is Too Much?　When is Too Soon?

One common guideline that is used on injuries is the simple rule of "let pain be your guide." Running or working through pain is rarely successful, because the person often exacerbates the condition, and then must decrease or abstain from activity until the problem is resolved. During rehabilitation, there is often pain associated with stretching out soft tissue and strengthening weak muscles. This, too, can be overdone. Part of the therapist's or trainer's education is to learn what are acceptable levels of discomfort that will be tolerated by their patients or athletes. Simply put, the pain of rehabilitation is experienced when the patient stops hurting shortly after the exercise is over, and they continue to improve. Pain of injury or reinjury is when the pain continues long past the activity, and the injury is worse the next day. Other signs such as decreases in range of motion or strength, or increases in swelling are indicators of too fast a progression in a rehabilitation program.

Finally, it would be a mistake not to give special attention to the use of the swimming pool as a rehabilitative device. Musculoskeletal injuries are often alleviated by work in a gravity reduced environment. The injured person may move in water with much less shock and effort. At the same time, if aerobic activity is indicated, the pool certainly can provide that. There are some examples such as shoulder, neck, or open wound problems when use of a pool is limited. However, the pool does provide a unique opportunity to remain active to many going through rehabilitation.

Summary

As with a lot of things in life, rehabilitation after a sports injury is complicated by the question of how much activity or treatment is too much, or too little. The line between too much and too little may be very fine. As the injured person responds to the rehabilitation, time, and rest since the injury, the activity tolerated will constantly change. The purpose of the information in this chapter was to provide some answers and philosophy for the challenge of working with an injured sports or activity participant.

Review Questions

1. List five goals of rehabilitation.

2. Give an example of how one could safely "work around" and injury during rehabilitation.

3. Give an example of what can go wrong when someone tries and fails to "work around" an injury.

4. Why is maintenance of aerobic training important during rehabilitation?

5. List some positive things that can be engaged in during rehabilitation of an injury.

6. Discuss the pros and cons of working on technique during an injury.

7. What are some guidelines regarding pain and recovery from an injury?

8. List four signs that indicate the rehabilitation process is being progressed too rapidly.

9. Discuss the advantages of the swimming pool for use in rehabilitation.

Suggested Readings

Arnheim, D. D. (1985). <u>Modern Principals of Athletic Training</u>. St. Louis: Times Mirror/Mosby College Co.

Curwin, S., & Standish, W. (1984). <u>Tendonitis: Its Etiology and Treatment</u>. Lexington: D. C. Heath and Co.

Nicholas, J. A., & Hershman, E. B. (1986). <u>The Lower Extremity and Spine in Sports Medicine</u>. St. Louis: C. V. Mosby Co.

O'Donaghue, D. H. (1984). <u>Treatment of Injuries to Athletes</u> (4th ed.). Philadelphia: W. B. Saunders Co.

Chapter 9

Drugs and Environmental Conditions Relating to Sports Injury

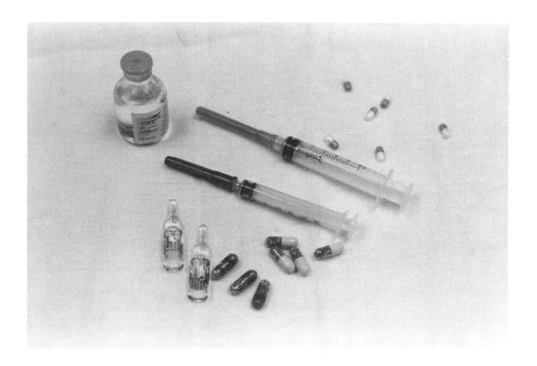

Introduction

The use of drugs in an attempt to enhance human performance has been present for centuries in a variety of cultures. Our problem today is that the awareness and availability, coupled with the willingness of people to use drugs to gain some perceived advantage, is increasing. The risks to health can be from either short or long term use. There are many documented cases of disqualifications and censorship from competition as well as devastating physical and mental side effects, and even death, among athletes who disuse and abuse drugs. Yet, the problems continue to grow. Survey studies have reported that 20% of intercollegiate athletes used steroids in three separate studies done in 1976, 1980, and 1984 (Pope et al., 1988). The purpose of this chapter is to review the major effects of drugs and ergogenic aides as they relate to the prevention of sports injury.

First, it should be emphasized that reliable research on the effects of many types of drugs is not available. For example, the studies on anabolic/androgenic steroids concentrate on strength, body mass and mental aggressiveness. However, there is a lack of research on the effects of drug use on soft tissues such as cartilage, ligament, and tendon. Even correlation studies which plot drug use with injury incidence is lacking because of the underground nature of the drug problem. There are good ethical reasons not to do a study where you have pro football players ingest known amounts of anabolic steroids during a season, and compare their injury rates to a control group. Even though dangers exist (see below), it is known that many athletes, whether professional or amateur, take anabolic steroids routinely.

Anabolic Steroids

Side Effects

Use of anabolic steroids, whether in continuous or cycle programs, have shown that liver damage can occur. Also, the athlete on anabolic steroids is putting the cardiovascular system in jeopardy because the low density lipo-protein levels increase and the high density lipo-protein levels decrease. The higher total cholesterol levels causes atherosclerosis. These individuals would many times be protected from high cholesterol levels due to their diet and exercise regimens. But, due to their drug use, instead of being protected, they are at significantly higher risk of diseases such as heart attack and stroke. Cardiac myopathy is another serious side effect of anabolic steroids. There have been cases recently in the literature which document this side effect causing illness and/or death (Telander & Noden, 1989).

Another side effect of anabolic steroid use is the hormonal balance changes which occur, and their resultant effects on an individual's sex characteristics. For example, the development of breast tissue and testicular atrophy in men, and facial hair in women, is a relatively common occurrence when anabolic steroids are used.

In recent years, many anabolic steroid using athletes have been attempting to reduce the side effects of cardiovascular, liver, and hormonal imbalances by adding other drugs. The addition of these drugs (sometimes called "stacking") is particularly dangerous because there is little known about the interaction of these drugs. Since they are not managed by a physician who would normally do clinical evaluation and laboratory tests to insure the therapeutic dose is not exceeded, the athlete is placed in even greater danger.

Injury

The relationship of anabolic steroid use and traumatic injury to the musculoskeletal system again is not well known. There are some anecdotal reports, but the literature is limited to a few case studies. One specific study reported the case of a 24-year-old power lifter who was 5 feet 8 inches tall and weighed 275 pounds. He was squatting 750 pounds in a warm up for a meet when he experienced "something give away" in both his knees causing him to fall down. It was discovered after hospitalization that he had completely ruptured the rectus femoris tendon on the left and had a partial tear of the rectus femoris tendon of the right knee. The man had taken a regimen of seven different drugs either orally or by intramuscular injection over a period of 10 weeks prior to the power lifting event and injury. The report also stated that "The subject was not under any medical supervision, although he was extremely knowledgeable about the potential side effects" (Hill et al., 1983).

Biomechanically, we do not know exactly why the injury happened. But, the muscle had a greater capacity to pull than the tendon had the capacity to tether the force between the muscle and the patella. Since the failure of the tendon happened in the warm-up, it might also be assumed that there was some pre-existing strain damage to the tendon that was caused by training in the weeks prior to the injury. Had the injury happened during a single maximum lift, one might suspect that the growth in strength of the muscle tissue simply outgained the tendon and there was no pre-existing tendon injury. But, even if you could determine whether or not the tendon was compensated before the actual rupture, there are too many variables in the case to figure out the exact cause. For example, which drug, in combination with what other drugs, and in what dose, combined with what specific training program?, are a few of the questions that need answering.

Behavior Changes

Another aspect of anabolic steroids which has not been discussed, but is important to the prevention of injury, is prevalence of emotional mood swings and, specifically, the aggressive behavior. An aggressive attitude toward hard work and competition has been rewarding to athletes in the past. However, it is easy to see how drug induced aggression can be a big problem as it impairs judgment both on and off the field.

Human Growth Hormone

One of the newest drugs that is being abused is synthetic human growth hormone or hGH. The US Olympic Committee has recently added hGH to the list of banned substances because of its potential for abuse. It is used by sports oriented youths who hope to grow bigger and stronger, as well as by mature adults who seek an increase in muscle mass much like the users of anabolic-androgenic steroids. At this time hGH is comparatively very expensive compared to anabolic steroids. However, if the synthetic production of this drug becomes less costly, it is feared that many more athletes and young people may use it thinking that it may be safer and have less side effects than steroids.

The side effects of hGH include acromegaly, or the abnormal growth of many organs, bones, and the facial features. Diseases such as diabetes, heart and thyroid disease, and decreased sexual drive are listed as related to hGH abuse. Muscle laxity is also a possible side effect. However, rather than equivocate on what specific system or organ may be affected, it does make sense to note a general truth about most of the hormonal manipulations that are the result of drug abuse. Whenever the body is artificially supplied with an overdose of a hormone, the body's natural production of that hormone is decreased or in some cases stopped. This goes for hGH and the anabolic-androgenic steroids as well (Cowart, 1988; Taylor, 1988).

Ergogenic/Ergolytic Drugs

Stimulants

A plethora of other drugs have been misused and abused to attempt some improvement in performance. They all have their problems which unfortunately make them ergolytic or performance inhibiting rather than ergogenic or performance enhancing.

The drugs that are considered stimulants are caffeine, amphetamines and even cocaine. They are used to mask or delay fatigue. The ergolytic side effects include agitation, tremors, insomnia, and anxiety. Other more serious side effects to the users of cocaine and amphetamines specifically include heart arrhythmia, hyperthermia, and cardiac failure. There have been several deaths of highly conditioned sports figures who have abused cocaine, just as there are deaths due to cocaine use by the general population.

Depressants

Anxiety reducing drugs include alcohol and barbiturates. Their ergolytic side effects include a slowing of reaction time, impaired balance, and reduced endurance. General health risks of liver disease, cardiovascular and neurological compensation also are present as a part of the negative side effects of alcohol abuse.

Beta-blockers are drugs sometimes used to reduce tremors in competitive marksman sports of shooting and archery. They also have side effects of hypotension, broncho-spasms and impotence. These drugs are used therapeutically to treat hypertension, angina, heart arrythymias and headaches.

Corticosteroids

The injection of corticosteroids to reduce inflammation and pain is a common practice. The overall effect on the tendon or ligament is, however, not always good. Tendons and ligaments injected with corticosteroids have a decrease in tensile strength. The collagen and ground substance formation is compensated, as is the surrounding circulation. There are cases of tendon rupture after repeated injection with corticosteroids and the resumption of activity. This is particularly difficult to handle clinically because the injection will decrease the pain, and the patient will want to return to activity before the recommended two to three week rest period has passed.

Another related problem with corticosteroid injection is that many times they are mixed with an anesthetic such as lidocaine or marcaine. Injection into muscle tissue has a myotoxic effect. (Carlson & Rainin, 1985; Foster & Carlson, 1980). The regeneration of the destroyed muscle tissue takes from one to two months. The return to activity after an injection of corticosteroids and anesthetic may, in fact, be slower than approaching a chronic inflammatory problem more conservatively and completely resting the injured part.

Sports Medicine Personnel

The challenge for the trainers, physical therapists, and physicians who attend to the athlete is to be aware of the side effects of all types of drugs which an athlete may use. Besides the recreational drugs, which athletes use at the same rate as the general population, there are many new drugs and new applications of old drugs and combinations of drugs which may be used in an attempt to improve performance in sports. This problem is complicated by the fact that many of these drugs are illegal or prohibited by sports governing bodies. Therefore, the athlete is not likely to voluntarily seek information from those who could really help him or her the most. However, the vigilant, realistic, compassionate, and informed sports medicine care giver is best prepared to prevent injury and incident to athletes and sports participants who use drugs.

Environmental Concerns During Sport/Exercise Activities

The human body has adapted quite comfortably to the environment in which it lives. However, there are times when the environment poses a threat to the well-being of an individual. Temperature extremes, heat and cold, affect the thermoregulatory system of the body. Moving in high altitudes, or submerging beneath the water away from the "normal" environment calls for certain adaptations to be made. These situations sometimes are compounded during the stress of sport or exercise participation. Four problem areas will be discussed in this section: heat, cold, altitude, and water submersion.

Heat Stress

The normal body temperature is 98.6°F (37°C), or a safe range of 91.6°F to 105.6°F. The hypothalmus gland, located in the brainstem, is the thermoregulator, or "thermostat" for the body. It senses changes in the internal temperature of the body via thermoreceptors found in various parts of the body (e.g. skin, peritoneal cavity, spinal cord, brainstem), or via the blood. If the body becomes overheated, the hypothalmus reacts by sending signals to the blood vessels causing vasodilation, or the sweat glands causing perspiration in an effort to cool the body down (Noble, 1986).

Mechanisms of Heat Loss

The key to body temperature control is to equalize heat production and heat loss to maintain normalcy. During activity, internal body temperatures are elevated. Body heat somehow must be dissapated to keep the body from overheating (>105°F). This can be done in several ways: (1) conduction, (2) convection, (3) radiation, and (4) evaporation. (See Table 9.1) The first three are considered to be passive mechanisms for heat dissiaption, while the fourth is considered to be an active mechanism.

Table 9.1. Mechanisms of Heat Loss in Moderate and High Air Temperatures. *

Air Temperature	Heat Mechanism	%Contribution
75	Conduction	0
95		0
75	Convection	10
95		6
75	Radiation	67
95		4
75	Evaporation	23
95		90

*Adapted from Noble, 1984.

Conduction.   Heat from a warm object is transferred to a colder object by direct surface contact. Only a small amount of body heat is lost in this manner, and almost none is lost during exercise or activity in high environmental temperatures.

Convection.   Heat loss under this mechanism occurs when the air is moving. Body heat is transferred to the moving air. Not much body heat can be dissipated via this method either, especially if there is no air movement. It becomes increasingly difficult to lose body heat as the environmental temperatures rise.

Radiation.   Under moderate temperatures (75°F, 24°C), body heat is lost via this mechanism more that any other method. As air temperatures rise, however, this source of heat dissipation becomes less prevalent.

Evaporation.   This mechanism of heat loss occurs when water from the skin and lungs is converted to a gaseous state. Approximately one-third of the evaporation occurs from the skin, while the remaining one-third is released from the lungs (Bangs, 1984). This method of heat loss occurs more frequently when air temperatures are high (e.g. 95°F).

Heat and Humidity

Internal body temperatures are elevated during exercise or physical activity. The problem becomes compounded when the external air temperatures are elevated, and especially when humidity accompanies the rise in temperatures. A Wet Bulb Globe Temperature (WBGT) Index is a tool designed to evaluate heat and humidity in the prevention of heat-related complications. It is a combination of readings from three thermometers giving dry, humid, and radiant heat indications. The three readings are combined in a standard formula which provides a more accurate reading of the stress intensity. (Physical Fitness Specialist Course Manual, Institute for Aerobics Research, 1979)

The formula for calculating the "effective temperature" or heat stress index was developed by the U. S. Armed Forces. It is as follows:

$$WBGT = 0.7 \times T^{wb} + 0.2 \times T^{g} + 0.1 \times T^{db}$$

where T^{wb} =   Temperature wet bulb thermometer
T^{g} =   Temperature black globe thermometer
T^{db} =   Temperature dry bulb thermometer

Another method of determining the heat stress index is to combine the figures for air temperature and relative humidity. (Institute for Aerobics Research, 1979) The chart may be found in Figure 9.1.

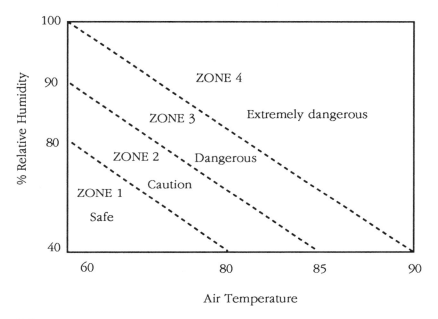

Figure 9.1.
Heat stress index. (Adapted with permission from the Physical Fitness Specialist Course Manual, Institute for Aerobics Research, 1979)

In general, any combination of relative humidity and air temperature adding up to 160 or less is considered to be safe for exercise and strenuous activity. Any combinination of humidity and air temperature which exceeds 190 is considered to be extremely dangerous.

Heat Problems

Three common problems exist when heat loss in the body cannot keep up with heat production. They are heat cramps, heat exhaustion, and heat stroke.

Heat Cramps. Heat cramps are characterized by painful spasms in the muscles, especially the legs or the abdomen. There are those who believe that heat cramps are the result of water and salt loss which are needed for normal muscle contractions. Others feel that an electrolyte imbalance causes the cramping. It is thought that heat cramps occur more frequently at the beginning of the heat season before acclimatization has occurred. (Ellison, 1984). They should not be confused with muscle cramps which generally are due to exhaustion. (See Table 9.2 for symptoms of muscle cramps).

Heat Exhaustion. The chances for heat stress increase on a hot, humid day, during times when the sun is direcly overhead, or when no wind is blowing. It develops when exercise/sport participants become dehydrated allowing the blood volume to drop. Increased blood flow is needed by the muscles and cardiovascular system to meet the demands of the stress imposed by the increased activity. The skin also needs additional blood flow to assist in the process of getting rid of the excessive heat the body has generated. A shortage is created and the peripheral vascular system collapses. The body goes into "shock" because it cannot cope with all of the demands. (See Table 9.2 for symptoms of heat exhaustion.)

Heat Stroke. Heat stroke is by far the most serious of the heat-related problems. Death is imminent if left untreated. In heat stroke, all of the body's cooling devices have failed. The evaporation mechanism for dissipating body heat shuts down. Body temperatures are elevated to extremely high levels. (See Table 9.2 for symptoms of heat stroke.)

Table 9.2. Signs and Symptoms of Heat-Related Problems.

Heat Cramps	Heat Exhaustion	Heat Stroke
Painful spasms	Profuse sweating	Hot, dry skin
Cool, moist skin	Cool, moist skin	Flushed skin
Normal temperature	Normal/low temperature	High temperature
Rapid pulse	Rapid, weak pulse	Rapid, pounding
Low blood pressure	Low blood pressure	pulse
	Weakness	Elevated blood pressure
	Dizziness	Delirious
	Headache	
	Nausea	

Prevention of Heat-Related Injuries

Prevention of heat-related injuries is basic. Some of the more common ways in which to avoid them are:

1. Be sure you are in condition to exercise vigorously or participate in a sport before the heat season. If you are not in condition, acclimatize yourself to the heat conditions by starting out slowly. Then follow a systematic progression of activity designed to increase intensity and duration.

2. Wear clothing which allows for the free flow of air and the dissipation of body heat.

3. Drink plenty of water. Small amounts should be taken prior to the exercise or activity. Then, if possible, fluids should be taken frequently during exercise or activity, and then continue to be taken after the bout has been terminated.

4. Check the weather reports prior to being active in heat conditions. Look on the WBGT Index for safe and risky conditions for participating in exercise or sport activities.

Cold Related Problems

When heat loss becomes greater than heat production, the body temperature drops. Generally, heat is lost through the same mechanisms as described under heat stress. Those mechanisms are radiation, convection, conduction, and evaporation. Temperatures that fall below the 90° F cause a disturbance in the functioning of the hypothalmus. The lower limit for survival is said to be around 74°F.

Physiological Response to Cold Temperatures

When the body core temperature drops below normal or the skin becomes cold, two responses occur in an attempt to decrease heat loss. First, the body closes down the circulation to the skin. This causes a loss of heat in this area so that more can be directed to the inner core of the body where the veins and arteries lie close to one another. The heat exchange between the two is a mechanism for conserving heat. Second, the body begins to shiver in an attempt to convert the energy from the shivering action to heat.

If heat loss continues to exceed heat production, the regulatory system fails. Respiration becomes difficult, and the heart may begin to fibrillate.

Cold Related Problems

Two major problems are related to overexposure to cold temperatures. They are hypothermia and frostbite.

Hypothermia.   A condition known as hypothermia develops when the core temperature of the body falls below 95°F. This can become an extremely dangerous situation, possibly death, if the temperature drops below 78°F (27.5°C). The major causes of hypothermia are sudden immersion into cold water, chronic exposure to the cold, wet clothing, and cold winds.

The initial reaction to being immersed in cold water is a gasp. This can lead to asphyxiation if the head is submerged. Following the initial gasp, there is a period of hyperventilation. This causes some confusion in the victim, obscures judgement, and may result in unconciousness. Muscles go into tetany which restricts movement. Although swimming increases heat production, it also causes more surface area to be exposed to the cold water. More surface area exposure drops the core temperature of the body more rapidly. (Bangs, 1984) See Figure 9.3 for a life expectancy table for cold water immersion supplied by the U. S. Public Health Service.

Hyperthermia also may be caused by overexposure to cold temperatures, wetness, and blowing winds. Hikers may start out walking in moderate temperatures (50°F) with warm clothing to protect them from the elements. As they perspire, they may remove some of their outer clothing. Cold winds and cold temperatures may react with the wet clothing to produce a hypothermic condition. The symptoms are much like those found in cold water immersion: (1) uncontrollable fits of shivering; (2) vague, slow, slurred and thick speech; (3) memory lapses, incoherence; (4) poor judgement; (5) frequent stumbling; (6) muscle rigidity and tenseness; (7) blueness of skin; (8) drowsiness; and (9) apparent exhaustion. (Hafen, 1981)

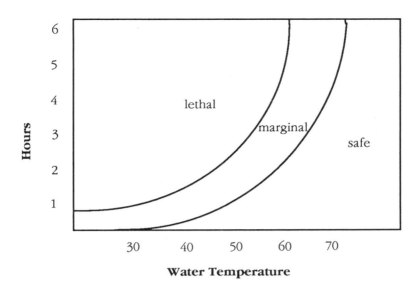

Figure 9.2.
Life expectancy for cold water immersion. Source: U.S. Public Health Service.

Frostbite.   Frostbite occurs with extreme exposure to cold temperatures. There are degrees of tissue damage depending upon the wind factor, temperature, humdity, and length of exposure. See Table 9.2 for wind chill factors.

Table 9.2.   Wind Chill Factors.

WIND (MPH)	\multicolumn{16}{c}{TEMPERATURE (FAHRENHEIT)}
0	35	30	25	20	15	10	5	0	-5	-10	-15	-20	-25	-30	-35	-40
							\multicolumn{9}{c}{Equivalent Chill Temperature}								
5	30	25	20	15	10	5	0	-5	-10	-15	-20	-25	-30	-35	-40	-45
10	20	15	10	5	0	-10	-15	-20	-25	-35	-40	-45	-50	-60	-65	-70
15	15	10	5	0	-10	-20	-25	-30	-40	-45	-50	-60	-65	-70	-80	-85
20	10	5	0	-10	-15	-25	-30	-35	-45	-50	-60	-65	-75	-80	-85	-95
25	15	0	-5	-15	-20	-30	-35	-45	-50	-60	-65	-75	-80	-90	-95	-105
30	5	0	-10	-20	-25	-30	-40	-50	-55	-65	-70	-80	-85	-95	-100	-105
\multicolumn{5}{c}{Little Danger}	\multicolumn{6}{c}{Increasing Danger}						\multicolumn{6}{c}{Great Danger}					

Source: Institute for Aerobics Research, 1979.

When the tissues of the body become chilled, ice crystals form in the fluids of the skin. As the crystals grow, they damage the underlying tissue. The areas of the body most frequently affected are the ears, nose, fingers, and toes.

The less severe form of frostbite causes redness, swelling, and a tingling sensation. No tissue damage occurs. The more severe forms of frostbite cause blisters, reddened skin, and edema. The most severe form of frostbite presents with a grayish appearance in the tissues. This is an indication that damage has occurred.

Prevention of Cold Related Problems

Cold related problems may be prevented by following several basic precautions:

1. Wear proper clothing. Wear layers of clothing. Be sure the outer layers of clothing are wind and water proof. Wear mittens for the hands and shoes or boots with lightweight cotton socks next to the skin.

2. Check the temperature, wind, and humidity before activity.

3. Be in good condition. Warmup properly and cool down slowly.

4. Eat adequately to compensate for increased metabolic rate.

5. Avoid alcohol and nicotine.

Altitude Sickness

At one time the only people who were susceptible to altitude sickness were those who lived or worked at high altitudes. That has changed with the emphasis in recreational activities such as mountain climbing, camping, skiing, and cycling. More people are "taking to the mountains" for the weekend to enjoy nature at its finest. These weekend trips, or any short-lived visit, to high altitudes pose a problem for those who do not have the time to become acclimatized to the thinner air. Symptoms may appear at 7,500 to 8,000 feet, and death has been known to occur at altitudes of 8,000 or 9,000 feet. (Ellison, 1984)

The major danger of moving in high altitudes is the lack of oxyen (hypoxia). Secondarily, are the dangers of cold temperatures and overexposure to the rays of the sun. The degree of risk is dependent upon: (1) speed of ascent; (2) altitude reached; and (3) length of stay.

Type of Altitude Sickness

Altitude sickness may vary from an acute bout resulting from a short stay at low altitudes to a chronic mountain sickness from living for long periods at high altitudes. Additionally, the degree of altitude sickness may vary from person to person. Three of the most common forms of altitude sickness are described below. (Houston, 1984)

Acute Mountain Sickness (AMS). This type of altitude sickness is found in those individuals who climb to relatively low altitudes of between 7,000 and 8,000 feet for one day of activity. Some of the common symptoms are headache, vomiting, nausea, light headedness, labored breathing, sleep disturbance, and fatigue. These symptoms usually occur anywhere from 6-96 hours after arriving at a given altitude. Generally, there are no long term lasting effects of acute altitude sickness. The symptoms normally clear away in two to five days.

High Altitude Pulmonary Edema (HAPE). HAPE occurs at higher altitudes of between 9,000 to 10,000 feet. At these higher altitudes, fluid accumulates in the lungs causing labored breathing, coughing, headache, weakness, and stupor. Often it occurs in individuals who have descended from this altitude and then have returned again to the higher altitude.

High Altitude Cerebral Edema (HACE). When altitudes between 10,000 to 12,000 are reached, the brain becomes affected. Persons who become ill at these heights experience severe headaches, hallucinations, weakness, muscular uncoordination, and emotional instability. Coma and death could result from long exposure to these conditions.

Prevention of Altitude Sickness

Altitude sickness may be prevented by conditioning the body for exercise at these heights prior to the actual event. Persons who are aerobically conditioned have higher altitude threshholds than those who do not.

The best overall preventative for altitude sickness is to control the rate of ascent. The next best preventatives are to control the length of stay and the altitude reached. It may be necessary to descend to lower levels periodically if a longer stay in the higher altitudes is contemplated. Descent to lower altitudes always is mandatory if symptoms of altitude illness are present.

Water Submersion Risks

The water environment poses a different set of risks for the water sport enthusiast. The two major conditions under which an accident is likely to occur are ascending and descending into deep water. The weight of the water as one descends into the deep causes an increase in atmospheric pressure upon the body. At sea level, there is one atmosphere of pressure exerted on the body. (1 atomosphere of pressure is defined as the weight of air pressing on the surface of the body at sea level.) When the body submerges to a depth of 33 feet, the atmospheric pressure increases two-fold. This causes a problem with the gas exchanges in the body.

Descending Into Deep Water.

Descending into deep water causes compression problems, especially in the middle ear. These compression problems, also referred to as "squeeze" problems, occur because the pressure is not equalized between the outside pressure and the pressure within the Eustachian tubes of the ear. Hemorrhaging may occur within the tympanic membrane, and blood may spill out into the cavity. If the tympanic membrane ruptures, cold water rushes into the ear causing disorientation in the diver. Other areas where the "squeeze" may occur are the lungs, sinus cavities, eyes, and nose.

Ascending from the Deep

More serious problems result from ascending to the surface. The two most dangerous problems are an air embolism and decompression sickness. As the pressure on the body decreases during ascent, gas within the lungs increases. This is in accordance with Boyle's Law which states: The volume of a confined gas whose temperature is held constant will vary in inverse proportion to the pressure on the gas. In the case of the ascending diver, an ascent from a depth of 33 feet to the surface will increase the volume of gas by 100 per cent.

Air Embolism. An air embolism is an air bubble which has been created by the expanding gas in the lungs. Lung tissue ruptures under the pressure causing the escape of air and damage to surrounding blood vessels. Bubbles caused by the escaping air are sent to various parts of the body where they may become lodged. The normal supply of blood and oxygen are restricted to these areas and may cause serious problems. If the embolism settles in the brain, the diver experiences symptoms similar to a stroke. Some of the signs and symptoms are numbness in the limbs or face, visual disturbances, bloody fluid at the mouth or nose, dizziness, difficulty in breathing, and paralysis.

Decompression Sickness. Decompression sickness results from being submerged in deep water for long periods of time. Deep-sea divers are more likely to encounter this condition than are scuba divers. It is caused by nitrogen bubbles being released into the blood. Underwater breathing causes more than the usual amount of air to be absorbed into the tissues. Eighty per cent of the air mixture is nitrogen while the other twenty per cent is oxygen and carbon dioxide. The oxygen and carbon dioxide diffuse rapidly throughout the body tissues, but nitrogen does not. It is released slowly in the form of bubbles which are carried by the blood throughout the body. If the diver ascends too rapidly, the nitrogen is released much more rapidly and the bubbles enlarge. This causes an obstruction in the blood vessels, or other tissues of the body if it is a severe case of decompression sickness. (Ellison, 1984).

Symptoms may appear immediately or after several hours. There is extreme pain in the joints causing the diver to "bend" over to gain relief. Hence, the term "bends" often is given to decompression sickness. If the air bubbles have affected the spinal cord, particularly in the throacic region, paralysis may result.

Prevention of Water Submersion Problems

Several precautionary measures should be taken before deciding to engage in underwater activities.

1. Check all equipment before attempting any diving activity.

2. Dive with a partner.

3. Know how to descend and ascend properly.

4. Limit the time and depth of the dive.

5. Be in good physical condition and free from any respiratory illnesses.

Summary

This chapter addresses two concerns of sport/exercise participants that are not concerned directly with the anatomical or biomechanical functions of the musculoskeletal system. Drugs are a major concern because of their use and abuse in organized sports, and in some cases, recreational sports. The most talked about drug problem of this decade is anabolic steroid usage. However, there are other drugs which may cause reactions after being used. Among them are the stimulants, depressants, human growth hormone, and corticosteroids. A knowledge of how they are used and possible side effects is essential to the well-being of the sport/exercise participant.

The environment produces another kind of stress on the body. Temperature changes may cause heat stress, hypothermia, or frostbite. Climbing to higher altitudes than what the body is accustomed to also may affect the respiratory system and brain adversely. Underwater submersion offers another potential risk for bodily harm in the form of "squeeze", air embolism, and decompression sickness. Knowing how the body reacts to these unusual environmental conditions is the first step in preventing these undesirable conditions.

Review Questions

1. Why is drug use among athletes attractive and why does the problem continue to become more complex?

2. What are the contra-indications of anabolic steroid use in general?

3. What biomechanical problems may arise from the use of anabolic steroids?

4. What are some dangerous side effects of cortico steroid and anesthetic injections?

5. What are the effects of so-called ergogenic drugs such as caffeine, cocaine, and amphetamines?

6. What are the general side effects of system depressants such as alcohol, barbiturates and also beta-blocker types of drugs?

7. Discuss why sports medicine personnel have a challenge in preventing drug related injuries?

8. What is the function of the hypothalmus gland?

9. Describe the 4 ways in which heat is lost from the body.

10. By what mechanism does the body lose heat when temperatures are moderate (75°)? High (95°)?

11. What is "effective temperature"?

12. What is the safest combination of air and humidity for exercising?

13. Distinguish between heat cramps, heat exhaustion, and heat stroke?

14. How can heat-related injuries be prevented?

15. How does the body respond to cold temperatures, physiologically speaking?

16. What are the major causes of hypothermia?

17. How do you know if someone has hypothermia?

18. How can hypothermia be prevented?

19. What happens, physiologically speaking, when frostbite occurs?

20. How do you know if frostbite has occurred?

21. How would you prevent frostbite from occurring?

22. The degree of risk for altitude sickness depends upon what 3 factors?

23. Distinguish between AMS, HAPE, AND HACE as far as altitude reached and body part affected?

24. How can altitude sickness be prevented?

25. Why does underwater submersion pose a threat to scuba divers or other water sport enthusiasts?

26. What causes "squeeze" problems in descending into deep water?

27. What is an air embolism? Why does it occur?

28. What is decompression sickness?

29. How can underwater submersion problems be avoided?

References

Bangs, C. C. (1984). Cold Injuries. In R. H. Strauss (Ed.). Sports Medicine (pp. 323-343). Philadelphia: W. B. Saunders Company.

Carlson, B. M., & Rainin, E. A. (1985, September). Rat extraocular muscle regeneration, Repair of local anesthetic-induced damage. Arch of Ophthalmology, 103, 1373-1377.

Cowart, V. (1988). Human growth hormone: The latest ergogenic aide? Physician and Sportsmedicine, 16(3), 175-185.

Ellison, Arthur E.,(Ed.). Athletic Training and Sports Medicine. Chicago: American Academy of Orthopaedic Surgeons, 1984.

Foster, A. H., & Carlson, B. M. (1980). Myotoxicity of local anesthetics and regeneration of damaged muscle fibers. Anesthesia Analog, 58.

Hafen, B. Q. (1981). First Aid for Health Emergencies. St. Paul: West Publishing Company.

Hill, J. A. (1983). The athletic polydrug abuse phenomenon: A case report. American Journal of Sports Medicine, 11(4).

Houston, C. S. (1984). Man At Altitude. In R. H. Strauss (Ed.). Sports Medicine (pp. 344-360). Philadelphia: W. B. Saunders Company.

Noble, B. J. (1986). Physiology of Exercise and Sport. St. Louis: Times Mirror/Mosby College Publishing.

Physical Fitness Specialist Course Manual. (1979). Dallas: Institute for Aerobics Research.

Pope, H. G., Katz, D. L., & Champoux, R. (1988). Anabolic-Androgenic steroid use among 1,010 college men. Physician and Sports Medicine, 16(7), 75-80.

Taylor, W. N. (1988). Synthetic human growth hormone: A call for federal control. Physician and Sportsmedicine, 16(3), 175-185.

Telander, R., & Noden, M. (1989). The death of an athlete. Sports Illustrated, February 20, 70-78.

Suggested Readings

1. American College of Sports Medicine. (1982). The use of alcohol in sports. Med. Sci. Sports Exerc., 14, 481-482.

2. Ranaud, A. M., & Cromier, Y. (1986). Acute effects of marijuana smoking on maximal exercise performance. Med. Sci. Sports Exerc., 18(6), 685-689.

3. Bracken, M. E., Bracken, D. R., Winder, W. W., & Conlee, R. K. (1989). Efforts of various doses of cocaine on endurance capacity in rats. J. Appl. Physiology, 66, 377-383.

4. Chich, T. W., Halperin, A. K., & Gacek, E. M. (1988). The effect of anti-hypertension medications on exercise performance: A review. Med. Sci. Sports Exerc., 20, 447-454.

5. Joyner, M. J., Freund, B. J., Jilka, S. M., Hetrick, G. A., Martinez, E., Euey, G. A., & Wilmore, J. H. (1986). Effects of beta blockade on exercise capacity of trained and untrained men: A hemodynamic comparison. J. Appl. Physiology, 60, 1429-1434.

6. Armstrong, L. E., Costill, D. L., & Fink, W. J. (1985). Influence of diuretic-induced dehydration on competitive recurring performance. Med. Sci. Sports Exerc., 17(4), 456-461.

7. Cohen, J. C., Noakes, T. D., & Spinaler Benolde, A. J., (1988). Hyper-cholesterolemia in male power lifters using anabolic-androgenic steroids. Physician and Sportsmedicine, 16, 4956.

8. Freed, D. L., Banks, A. J., Longson, D., et al. (1975). Anabolic steroids in athletics: Crossover double blind trial on weight lifters. British Medical J., 2, 471-473.

9. Lamb, D. R. (1989). Anabolic steroids and athletic performance. In Hormones in Sport, Z. Laron, A. Royal (Eds.), Rome: Serono.

10. Wilson, J. D. (1988). Androgen abuse by athletes. Endocrine Review, 9, 181-199.

11. Special report on drug testing. (1988). Physician and Sportsmedicine, 16(2).

12. Estep, R. (1986, October). The curse of cocaine. Muscle and Fitness, 47.

13. Chaikin, T., & Telander, R. (1988, October 24). The nightmare of steroids. Sports Illustrated.

Index

Appendix A

Muscular System
(Anterior and Posterior)

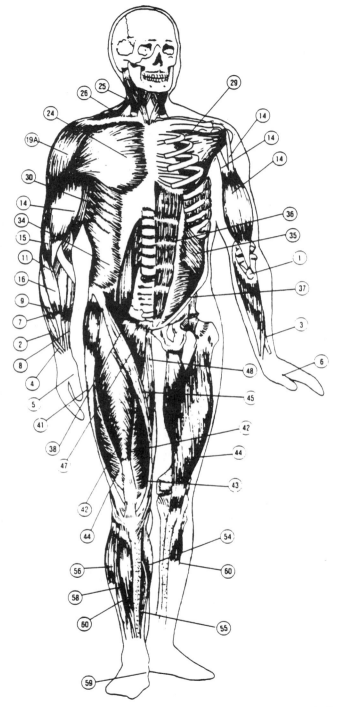

MUSCLE

1. Flexor Digitorum Profundus
2. Extensor Digitorum
3. Flexor Pollicis Longus
4. Extensor Pollicis Longus
5. Abductor Pollicis Longus
6. Adductor Pollicis
7. Flexor Carpi Radialis
8. Flexor Carpi Ulnaris
9. Extensor Carpi Radialis Longus and Brevis
10. Extensor Carpi Ulnaris
11. Pronator Teres
12. Pronator Quadratus
13. Supinator
14. Biceps Brachii
15. Brachialis
16. Brachioradialis
17. Triceps Brachii
18. Anconeus
19. Deltoid
   A. Anterior fibers
   B. Posterior fibers
20. Supraspinatus
21. Infraspinatus
22. Teres Minor
23. Teres Major
24. Pectoralis Major
25. Sternocleidomastoid
26. Trapezius
27. Splenius Cervicis/Capitus
28. Major and Minor Rhomboids, Levator Scapulae
29. Subscapularis

Anterior view of muscular system. (Reprinted by permission of Cramer Products, Inc., Gardner, Kansas.)

0. Serratus Anterior
1. Erector Spinae
2. Latissimus Dorsi
3. Quadratus Lumborum
4. External Abdominal Oblique
5. Internal Abdominal Oblique
6. Rectus Abdominus
7. Transversus Abdominus
8. Iliopsoas Pectineus
9. Gluteus Medius
0. Gluteus Maximus
1. Tensor Fasciae Latae
2. Rectus Femoris
3. Vastus Medialis
4. Vastus Lateralis
5. Sartorius
6. Adductor Magnus
7. Adductor Longus
8. Gracilis
9. Biceps Femoris
0. Semimembranosus
. Semitendinosus
. Popliteus
. Plantaris
. Gastrocnemius
. Soleus
. Peroneus Longus
. Peroneus Brevis
. Extensor Digitorum Longus
. Extensor Hallicus Longus
. Tibialis Anterior
. Tibialis Posterior
. Flexor Digitorum Longus
. Flexor Hallicus Longus

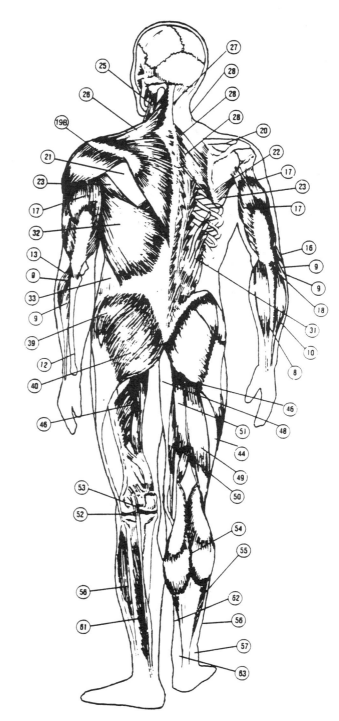

Posterior view of muscular system. (Reprinted by permission of Cramer Products, Inc., Gardner, Kansas.)

Notes